GENERATION ZERO

GENERATION ZERO

Reclaiming My Parents' American Dream

SABREET KANG RAJEEV

LIONCREST

PUBLISHING

GENERATION ZERO

Reclaiming My Parents' American Dream

ISBN   978-1-5445-1716-2 *Hardcover*

978-1-5445-1715-5 *Paperback*

978-1-5445-1714-8 *Ebook*

My parents

I have your prayers written all over me. Every word I speak, every thought I write will always start with you. Because of you, I am. Because I am, we are. Together and always.

My brother

Thank you for listening to me while becoming your own person at the same time. I know I am your older sister, but I am so proud of you. You are my pride and joy. You are so much greater than you may ever realize, and for everything you do, I'll always be your biggest fan.

My husband

Thanks for helping me realize that I can be understood. Your love for me never goes unnoticed. Without you, this book would have never been possible. I am a better woman because of you.

My chosen parents

Your kindness has no bounds. Thank you for loving me as if I had been with you since the day I was born. Your love shows me that humanity is good and how to love every being with open arms.

My unborn children

You deserve a model of love, not a martyr of love. I can't wait to love you for everything you were born to be.

My readers

This one is for you. I see you. I feel your pain. I know your suffering. I know our community can be better. Change starts with you.

CONTENTS

*Khudi ko kar buland itna, ki khuda bande se
khud puche, bata teri raza kya hain?*

*Make yourself so selfless, that one day God comes
down to ask you—what is it that you desire?*

—MUHAMMAD IQBAL

INTRODUCTION

APRIL 25, 1990 WAS THE DAY MY FATHER TOOK DOWN THE picture of Guru Nanak Dev Ji from the walls of his one-bedroom apartment in Flushing, Queens.

April 25, 1990 was also known as my birthday. I was born to an Indian taxi driver and his wife in Queens, New York. My father was so upset that I was born a girl, he literally became mad at God. He asked Waheguru:

Why did you give me a girl first? I've never asked anything of you. The only thing I have ever asked in my life was to give me a firstborn son and you, you disrespected me.

It's not that my father didn't want a daughter. He was okay with the thought of having a girl; he just didn't want a daughter *first*, and he didn't want multiple daughters. One was enough—if she was the second child.

Having a daughter first meant she would not continue the family name. It meant that it would be more expensive to raise her in America. It meant that she would move in with her in-laws after she was married and would not take care of him and his wife in their old age. Being the eldest meant that she didn't have an older brother with authority to look after her as she grew up. It meant that she wasn't protected, and she was all alone. Having a daughter is not an economically rational decision in the South Asian community. The difference between being born a daughter in India versus America—*I could live*. Being born a daughter meant I was unwanted. I was born without a voice. A voice that didn't matter because of my gender.

The truth is, the voicelessness that follows a female South Asian child from birth leaves millions of first- or second-generation women speechless, underestimating their potential and, ultimately, living a life filled with unprocessed trauma in their bodies. Being born into an immigrant family, the challenges an individual can face are often experienced in isolation. The collective trauma a family feels is silenced and understood as the necessary training wheels of assimilation. To further exacerbate our identities, there is no universal consensus on whether you can call yourself a first-generation or second-generation American to describe your family's or your immigrant experience.

According to the US Census Bureau, "first-generation" is the first family member to gain permanent residency in America. The Bureau also explains that "first-generation" can refer to individuals who were born outside of the United States. "Second-generation" refers to those with at least one parent who was born outside of the United States. Third- and fourth-generations include people who have two United States-native parents. Webster's New World Dictionary states that "first-generation" refers to a person who is the first in a family to be born a citizen of the country their family has relocated to. To complicate things further, it also states that people who immigrated over can be considered first-generation Americans after they gain legal residence.

I thought looking up the definition would help me understand if I was worthy of being an American (because I still felt unworthy as an Indian due to my gender), but it did not. I realized that as an individual of an immigrant family, understanding my generational status was as complex as understanding my own identity. I felt isolated because of my gender, and growing up, the differences I saw between my family and other South Asian immigrant families felt peculiar. I felt secluded from the only acceptable identity I could relate to in America and found myself withdrawn from the family who was given to me at birth. The picture of Guru Nanak Dev Ji went up fourteen months later after my brother was born. Growing up, my life was a constant reminder of why I am less and my brother was more. It is hard to believe in gender-equality when the first story you remember as a child is that your gender made your father upset.

Why did my gender matter? There must be something wrong with me. I must be the most well-behaved daughter, so my parents can love me.

In reality, it doesn't matter how my parents felt about me; what truly mattered were the internal battles they were suffering from when I arrived in this world. My father didn't want a daughter first because he knew that my voice would be hard to hear in the South Asian community. My father didn't want a daughter first because it meant he had to keep going to forge his 401(k) retirement plan (my brother). My father and mother didn't feel Indian or American; they just felt like martyrs of their family, looking to provide a better future to their lineage. They didn't consider themselves as any generation.

My family didn't feel like a first- or second-generation family. We felt like a family that started off at zero. *Generation Zero.* Throughout my life, I have struggled to understand the place my family has in American society. My parents came to this country with nothing. They started out at the bottom of the American class system, completely at zero. They had me and my brother here, giving us the greatest gift of all: American citizenship. We grew up and experienced the beauty of America together but in our own different and beautiful ways. We learned how to be both Indian and American separately. We grew to appreciate the grit we developed as a first-generation immigrant family. No matter how hard we worked as a family, we remained at zero because we weren't the stereotypical "Smart Indians." Everywhere we went, every book we read, every job we applied to, every place we stayed, we silenced our experiences because we felt culturally unworthy to be considered Indian or American.

This book was written to represent communities that are invisible to the mainstream South Asian immigrant experiences. For most of my life, I searched to find the meaning of my family's immigration history. The more I read, the more I realized that I was looking to find a story that gave me a sense of belonging. I read books that ranged from extraordinary to the most ordinary of tales. The more I searched, the emptier I felt. I was looking for a story to show me how to be a female in an immigrant American family. I yearned to find other struggling blue-collar families pouring their souls into their children. I tried to find other children striving to accomplish their parents' abandoned dreams in America. I looked and searched everywhere, but I always came up short. I slowly began to realize that the story that I desperately sought after was like my own. I am writing this book now because I finally have the strength to let other females in immigrant families know that they are not alone. There is a great deal of beauty and strength in belonging to an immigrant family. I come from one, and together, we were all once *Generation Zero*.

Part I

ADVENTURING TO AMERICA

SEARCHING

TWO PAIRS OF PANTS. TWO T-SHIRTS. THE SOCKS AND shoes he wore. His life savings of one thousand dollars. That is what my father brought to America at the age of twenty-three. No suitcase. No degree. Just whatever he could physically wear.

My father's journey to America is both odd and heroic. He traveled on a cargo ship. He was hired to clean the ship's oil room. Within a month of working, he was promoted to the ship's oil boy. There were thirty other workers on the ship with him. Some of them he knew; some of them he had met for the first time. The reason my father started working was to help his family back home in Punjab, India. My father is from the Jigerda caste. His family owned most of the land in Khamanon. He comes from a long line of agricultural, land-owning elites, who owned the land that farmers worked on. Jigerdas were kind to the people who worked for them and saw them as an extension of their family. My father was one of five children. He had an older brother and three sisters, and he was the youngest child. His father was a well-respected official, who unfortunately experienced the downfall of the farming industry after India gained its independence from the British in 1947.

Even though farming was once a lucrative business, it started declining in royalties, and all the luxuries that went along with the business (servants and drivers) started to disappear. The family was slowly losing their inheritance and started to struggle financially. To help, my father's older brother was forced to be an adult at a young age and looked everywhere to bring in money for his family. When you live in a third-world country, the dream always starts abroad. My uncle had found a job on a cargo ship first and now resided in America. My father dropped out of college to follow in the footsteps of his older brother. He looked to see if he could get a job on the ship simply because they paid in American dollars.

When he finally got the job, he was exhilarated. My father's first trip allowed him to see parts of the world he could have never imagined. He saw Singapore, Russia, China, Switzerland, Egypt, France, and even the United States. The ship would carry different supplies to different parts of the world. He would work day and night and be allowed to briefly go to shore at whichever location the ship docked. The crew was given little money to buy supplies before they were to board the ship again to go back to sea. On the voyage back home, my father was paid in cash as he left the ship. When he finally came home after his first trip, he brought his sisters some hairpins, his father a bottle of Johnnie Walker Black Label, and one lakh Indian rupees in 1984.

My father's second voyage was more familiar; he now knew what was expected of him. He knew that his trip was going to last around twelve months. He knew where they were going to stop. He started making friends and memorizing the maps of each country they went to (they were displayed all over the ship). He became aware that people had different tactics to leave the ship if they arrived at a destination they wanted to move to. He saw people using the ship's dinghy to go to shore while the ship waited idly to approach the dock. He admired their bravery and their stupidity for leaving all the money they earned behind. He became curious and wondered if he had the courage to maybe one day take the biggest risk of his life, too, by leaving the ship illegally.

When he arrived home from his second trip, he was told by his family that they had found a girl for him to marry. A woman who had a master's in English and could help him if he ever decided to leave the ship and go to America. My father didn't know if he wanted to get married just yet since he had his heart broken recently, but he decided to give the proposal a shot because sometimes, you never know how things are going to turn out. When he saw her picture, he was speechless. She was the most beautiful woman he had ever seen. It was love at first sight, and he told his family that if he were going to marry someone, it would only be her.

So, here is where my parents' story began. My father slowly started dreaming of going to America, and my mother had a master's in English and could help if he ever got there. A perfect combination for an arranged marriage destined for the States. My parents got engaged in 1984, right before my father left for his third voyage, where he planned on leaving the ship to go to America.

HIDDEN HEROES

PUNJAB HAS ONE OF THE LOWEST LITERACY RATES IN INDIA.
Literacy grew very slowly until India gained its independence
in 1947 and then gradually trended upward. In Punjab, literacy rates were exceptionally low because the main source of
income was agriculture. Punjab supplies most of the food for
India. In a traditional agricultural economy, education is not a
priority; it's for leisure. Only the elite Punjabis were educated.
Punjab has a class system that is defined by occupations. The
upper classes own land, and the rest of the classes participate
in agricultural jobs like farming, cleaning, and being servants
to wealthier households.

Most of Punjab practices Sikhism. Sikhism began with five
voluntary individuals known as *Panj Pyare*. The Panj Pyare practiced Hinduism and Islam and agreed to be baptized or *Amrit
Sanchar* into their new identities of Singh or Kaur. The reason
being that they believed in *Ek Onkar*, or in one universal God.
Sikhism teaches that all religious traditions are valid because they
all lead to the same *Waheguru* (God). To *Amrit Sanchar* and become a
Sikh means to believe in a casteless, democratic society. It means
to help and protect people in need. It means that regardless of
which religion you practice, we are all the same and have one
true God together. It was the first religion of its kind to say that

women have the same souls and rights as men. Guru Nanak Dev Ji indicated, "We are born of woman; we are conceived in the womb of a woman; we are engaged and married to a woman. Why should we talk ill of her, who gives birth to kings?" But even if equality is the founding pillar of your religion, it cannot control culture. In Punjabi culture, the caste system still exists, and women are not treated equally.

My mother is from the Jatt caste. She came from a family of businessmen who ran the first bus business in Calcutta. Her family was educated elites who came from Narangwal. Due to a few poor business decisions, the family lost their inheritance. Even though her father was well educated, they were down on their luck and could not afford to survive on their own. My mother was the firstborn child in her family. Because she was the eldest daughter, she grew up with a strong personality and was known to pave her own path to take care of herself and her family. Like many South Asian women, as soon as she was born, she was told that her only purpose was to serve her parents until she got married. Her parents had another girl and then eventually a son.

My mother's upbringing was far from easy. They never had enough food at home. She would pretend she was full of water so that her younger brother and sister could eat. She and her siblings grew up apart from each other. They grew up in different family member's homes who took them in to help raise them. Even though she came from a poor family, her extended family provided her an education, and she graduated with a master's in English from Punjab University. In college, she felt so affected by sexism that she led a march for women's rights. When my mother completed her studies, she was told that it was time to find her a suitor that her father approved of.

Since my mom was educated, her father was looking to find her a good and advantageous match who was moving abroad. He found her a man who was in pursuit of America. He came from a good, respectful family that owned land. The only problem was that he was not as educated as she was. My mother pleaded with her father to find someone educated, so they had something in common. She was quickly reminded that she was a daughter and that her family knew what was best for her. As a daughter, she did not have the right to say, "No." Her parents were trying to find her a husband who had the best financial future and chance of prosperity. In the end, my mother obeyed because of her unwavering love and truth in her parents. She felt obligated to listen to everything they wanted. Even though she had a great education, her cultural obligations made her believe she had no choice in how she could live her life, so she agreed to meet and marry their chosen suitor.

The aspiration of America, and what America really is, are two completely different ideas. Looking back at the history of immigration, America opened its hearts to foreigners, sometimes. During the Colonial era, large numbers of young men and women from Europe, Spain, and France crossed into the land of the free. In the mid-nineteenth century, Northern/Western Europeans, Germans, and Asians came to America. The Civil Rights Movement brought awareness about racist policies and pushed Congress to pass the Immigration and Nationality Act of 1965 due to the work of Black America. Post-1965, Asians could come to America because there was a nationwide shortage of doctors and other white-collar professions. Asians who were not educated could come to America only if they had money to invest in different businesses and properties. Put simply, the wealthy or educated South Asian had a slightly easier path to America, whereas the poor, uneducated South Asian was at the mercy of being given a shot at the dream.

Why would anyone ever leave a land their family has lived in for centuries? To escape their current reality? To provide a better financial future for their family? Why would anyone want to leave the only place they have ever called home?

To be heroes to their own families. My mother needed to provide stability for her family; the only way she knew how was by marrying a man going to America. My father wanted to show his family that he could be a responsible man by leaving the country and making money to help take care of his family in India. The dream to provide financial security always starts abroad. When an individual chooses to leave the only home they have ever known, sacrifices are calculated, and trade-offs are examined as a necessary offering to provide financial and familial peace of mind. To emigrate, you choose to miss life moments. You choose to disaffiliate from your family out of love. You choose someone else's happiness, every single day—someone else's peace of mind besides yours. Every dollar you make, every opportunity you chase isn't for you alone. The last thing you want to do as an immigrant is to let your sacrifice of self be in vain. To become an immigrant, you choose to be a hidden hero, day after day.

DREAMING OF FREEDOM

WHEN MY FATHER BOARDED THE SHIP FOR HIS THIRD VOYAGE, he knew it was going to be the last journey he would ever take. He had made up his mind that he was going to stop in America. He told his family and his new fiancé ahead of time. He brought with him his life savings and packed clothes he was comfortable leaving behind because he could not take his book bag off the ship; people would get suspicious. This trip felt different. He felt so many emotions simultaneously. Every place the ship docked was pleasant, but it was not America. He heard stories about the land of the rich and the strong-willed. He would study the American map and dream about the jobs America had.

What does freedom smell like? What does it feel like in the morning when you wake up? At night when you walk home from work? When you go to the super-market? What do people of freedom look like? Are they kind? Are they happy? Are they always smiling? America, America—oh, America. What can you offer an immigrant like me?

These thoughts occupied my father's mind at sea. He pre-pared himself, mentally and physically, every day until the time would be right for him to take the biggest risk of his life. He knew he would be ready when the moment came. He just had to believe. He was training his mind to believe.

His bravery and courage took the best of him one day. In the engine room, he overheard the captain talking about how he needed help sailing the ship. The captain was willing to provide direction to the sailor; he just needed someone who knew how to do the job. My father accidentally blurted out, "I can help sail. Let me know if you need my help." The captain agreed immediately and told him to come tomorrow night to help sail the ship from France to the United States. Back in his sleeping corridor, he told his friends what had happened:

Father: *Why did I blurt out that I know how to sail the ship? I have no idea how I'm going to do it, but I guess it can't be that hard. It's like driving a tractor, right?*

His friends: *You're pagal (crazy). How are you going to get out of this?*

Father: *I can't! They'll fire me.*

His friends: *Just pretend you are rusty, and you need some help. They'll help you.*

That's exactly what my father did. The following evening, he went into the command room confident in his ability to succeed, even though he had no professional training in sailing. The captain showed him how to steer the ship and started showing him the map and the path they were going to follow. *I can do this,* my father thought as he took a deep breath and started sailing the ship slowly, quietly, and convincingly, as if he was truly a sailor. He was courageous to the point of madness, able to clamber over any obstacle and make even the impossible true. As the weeks progressed, he was the on-call sailor. If there was a thunderstorm coming, a canal, anything that looked remotely dangerous, the captain would call for Singh to help sail the ship. With a smile and the will to succeed, my father always agreed to gracefully sail to the only dream he knew: America.

UNANNOUNCED "LOVE"

BEING ON THE SHIP WAS LONELY. EVEN THOUGH HE WAS working all hours of the day, my father's mind was always free to think and miss whomever he wanted. Being engaged changed who he daydreamed about. He missed his new fiancé more than he wanted to admit. He had fallen in love with her, even though he knew he wasn't allowed to before he married her. In arranged marriages, love comes after, not before. He loved how attentive she listened to him; how she believed in his dreams more than he did. She respected him. She made him feel like the man he wanted to become. He knew what risk he was putting her through because he had three sisters of his own. Indian daughters carry the weight of their family's reputation. That reputation is tied closely to when and whom they marry. Leaving an engaged woman behind, he knew that his fiancé's family was worried about one thing: what if their engagement fell apart? The strain that would have on her reputation was unbearable to think about.

What if I can't go back to India to marry her?

To escape that guilt, he put his head down and focused on the only obtainable goal he had in front of him on the ship. Everything seemed like a dream to him—how much she loved him and how he wanted to live in America. Fantasy was the only thing keeping him alive. He prayed that the fantasy he had of marrying the love of his life was closer to reality.

My mother was slowly fading away in India. Even though her marriage was arranged, she started to fall in love with her future husband. It happened gradually, and then all of a sudden when she realized she wouldn't be able to see or talk to him because he was going to America. His courage was contagious. His ability to listen and make her feel seen gave her a sense of hope; it made her feel alive. He was always respectful and gave her the ability to desire a life far away from here. But as each day passed, she grew concerned...

What if he never comes back? What if he forgets about me? When will I hear from him again?

She grew antsy. She knew what would happen to her family and her reputation if she never heard from him again. People would question her character, which would impact her whole family, including her unwed younger brother and sister. Waiting for him meant that she was putting everyone in jeopardy. Deep down in her core, she knew he was the right decision. If they could conquer this, they could conquer anything. Her family began to worry and told her that maybe they could find someone locally for her to marry. Determined, she rejected every opposition and stuck to what she knew to be true. She knew that everything was going to be okay, no matter how much time passed. She learned to silence her apprehension and believe blindly. She closed her eyes to think back to the last time she saw him. Her heart missed him, more than she could even understand. Before he left, he would write letters to her and leave them in front of her house. Now, she didn't have any letters to remind her of what he was like. All she had were the memories he left her with. For the next six months of her life, she patiently waited for a letter every single day.

UNWAVERING FAITH

MY FATHER BOARDED THE SHIP WITH ONE FAMILIAR FACE from his town, who was planning on making the trip to America with him: his brother-in-law. Even though his brother had told him how to escape the ship carefully so that he would not get caught, he still felt nervous. It's hard to calm your nerves when you have heard the horror stories of people unable to escape safely. If you get caught by the Americans when you arrive onshore, you'll be imprisoned (but you're still in an America jail). Getting caught by the staff and captains on the ship is harder because your dreams instantly die. Any violation means you lose your right to work on the ship, and you are sent back to the country you came from immediately. You lose your sense of purpose and your dream to provide for your family. If my father got caught by the staff on the ship, he would lose everything, including my mother's hand in marriage. When the stakes are higher than your dreams, it's impossible not to be agitated. You die slowly, each day, because you are constantly replaying what that risk will cost you in your life. The obstacle my father had to conquer as he slowly approached America was that fear. The fear of burying a life before he even had one.

On this trip, my father brought extra money with him because he knew he was going to leave behind the money he was earning. He had enough money to cover his living expenses in America, but my father's heart was too big to hold inside his chest. He met a man on the ship and desperately wanted to change his fate. It was his first trip, and he was having a difficult time adjusting to the reality that he would never be anything more than what he was that day. He was broken, without hope, even though there was an endless opportunity right in front of him. This man was crippled with the reality he left behind in India, his broken family. My father empathized with his burdens; they seemed a lot larger than his own. Without knowing him and expecting anything in return, he offered to give him some of his life savings, but only if he was willing to go with him on his adventure to America. No strings attached. He did not want the money back. My father just wanted him to be happy and believe in himself as much as he believed in him. Overcome with emotion, the man thanked him for taking a chance on him and asked if he could bring his friend too, to which my father responded, "Yes, only if you both believe in working hard."

After months of traveling, the ship finally arrived at a port in New Orleans, Louisiana. Here was the moment that could change my father's whole life. He had to be careful. Every move had to be perfect and calculated. He needed to look and act natural. He told his brother-in-law and his new friends to get ready.

Do not bring anything. Just whatever you can wear. Do not worry about your belongings; America will take care of us.

They were going to leave as soon as the postal guard was leaving for the day. That would give them enough time to quietly sail onto the shore. As the sun was setting, my father started to grow impatient.

Father: *We can jump in the water. I think it will be fine. We will use the nylon rope they use to anchor the ships at dock. If it can hold the ship, it can help us float in the water. Someone must throw it hard enough into the ocean that it's close enough to the shore. The shore is right there. We are so close. We can use the rope to help us float.*

Other men: *The rope will sink to the ocean floor! It's meant to anchor the ship! It's the Mississippi River! The waves are ruthless, and there are alligators and sharks in there.*

Father: *Do not worry; God is with us.*

Other men: *No, we will die! We don't know how to swim.*

Father: *Okay, okay, okay. We'll wait.*

When the sun had completely disappeared, the postal guard packed up his stuff and left for the day. Quickly, my father and his group got into the dinghy and paid one of the ship workers to reel them down. There was no going back. This was their only chance at the American dream. They descended slowly until they finally touched the sea. *Almost there.* The hardest part was ahead of them: rowing to the shore. The four of them worked hard to get the boat moving as quickly as they could. In the back of their minds, they all shared the same thought: *none of them knew how to swim.* If they started thinking they were dead men, then that was exactly what they were going to be. The waves were unmerciful. They feared that the boat would capsize, and they would be forced into the water to their sudden deaths. Trying to row faster (so they could get onshore without getting caught), they remained positive until they finally arrived at the shore. They disembarked. Reaching down to touch the soil, my father smiled.

America, the land of perpetual hope. I am here.

I grew up learning the story of how my father came to America. When he would tell me these stories as a child, it felt like a dream. Why do people come to America? There are other countries out there besides this one. Why this one? As a child, I couldn't understand his struggle, but as I grew into an adult, I was amazed by his bravery. The more educated I became, the more I realized just how incredible his journey truly was. I will never have a strong heart like my father. He bravely searched abroad to become the hidden hero his family needed by chasing the idea of freedom, accepting an unannounced arranged love, and having unwavering faith in his ability to achieve the American dream. He gravely believed that everyone could change their fate. He believed that he could be anything his heart desired because he controlled his destiny. Time after time, whenever he saw another immigrant weakened by their own self-doubt, my father taught them the courage to dream. His determination is the reason I believe in the American dream.

Part II

FINDING LIBERTY

INTOXICATED PURPOSE

ARRIVING IN AMERICA WAS INTOXICATING. EVERY ONE OF the men felt it. Imagine feeling invincible and afraid at the same time. That same feeling you feel before you are about to get on a roller coaster. My father started his journey by getting on the biggest roller coaster life had to offer him: completely starting over. Stepping off the ship, he chose to embrace a new identity: being an illegal immigrant. He knew he had to stay hidden and be invisible. He was ready to work harder than he had ever worked in his life because he wanted America to be his home.

What is the worst thing that could happen to me? Lock me up in an American jail? At least I am here. Free. With a dream.

America seemed friendly to him. He heard stories of the great country's generosity and kindness from strangers. He hoped to feel that hospitality one day. America is built on a dream—a dream that can be achieved if you work hard. He wanted to be anything that would allow him to stay here forever, which was why he was going to New York. New York is the city that never sleeps, full of life and chances. Not only was New York the ideal destination for an illegal immigrant; it was also where his brother lived.

As soon as my father stepped foot in New Orleans, he sat on a bench with his new friends to process what just happened. They were in America. They took a collective deep breath...followed by silence. The most painful part of the journey was over. The next step was getting a cab to the airport to get a ticket to New York City. His brother told him that people don't check your ID if you have enough money to make them look away. Listening to his brother's advice, my father had packed enough money to make sure officials would look away. After waiting for about half a day for the right flight, my father was on a plane to New York. If he could make it there, he could make it anywhere. He took a deep breath and closed his eyes, asking Waheguru to give him strength. *I just want to be an American. Please give me the opportunity to be one.* Within minutes, he fell asleep because his body was exhausted from being awake for more than twenty-four hours. When he awoke, he was in his new reality—New York City!

VOICELESS

THE FIRST THING EVERY IMMIGRANT LOOKS FOR IS A JOB.
My father was looking for an employer who understood that he
was an illegal immigrant. He went door to door, looking for a
job that was under the table. He committed to come to work
every day if that's what the business needed. Eventually, he found
a job as a meat stock clerk and was thrilled he finally had the
opportunity to start making money. He felt like he was on the
right path; he hoped that because he had a job, this meant he
could work toward getting his green card. As the weeks went by,
he started adjusting to his new life in America.

It was after my father arrived in America that he began writing to my mother again. After work, he would rush home to see
if he had any letters from India. The letters kept him alive and
gave him a reason to keep working hard. There would be days
where he would come home overwhelmed with emotion and
self-doubt. It was during those moments where he would pick
up a pen and pour out the words he was afraid to speak out loud.
With tears running down his face, he would write in Punjabi just
how hard life was without her. He closed his eyes and wished she
were with him. Maybe he would feel less alone then. It's hard
being alone. Being invisible, isolated, and scared is an aspect of
the American dream he wasn't prepared to battle.

* * *

One magical day, my mother received a letter that had postage from a country she did not recognize. It was addressed to her in my father's writing. She immediately ripped open the envelope. It was a pack of letters from him. Finally! She had been waiting for over six months to hear from him.

She raced through the letters; she was smiling, then crying, then angry, upset, and full of love. He was telling her about his journey to America and finally being there. Some days he seemed happy and optimistic, and on other days, she saw the tears he left on the page as he wrote how scared and alone he felt. He wrote whatever poetry he knew. He wrote whatever he was thinking because she was all he had. Her heart sank. She couldn't imagine how America looked, but she could feel how it made him feel. She decided that she would write back to him every single day. He needed her...and he was her destiny.

PERSEVERANCE

FOR THE NEXT YEAR, MY FATHER TIRELESSLY WORKED SEV-eral under-the-table labor jobs, but no one could promise him a green card. All his jobs were under his pen name, Singh. He was afraid of using his full name because he didn't want to be seen as a foreigner and sent back to India. Nobody wants to be sent back to a country they chose to leave. No one.

My father's first act of invisibility was adopting his Sikh middle name, Singh, as his last name. By dropping his last name, Kang, he was erasing his family identity and blending in with the rest of the Sikh immigrants in America. Your family's identity is everything in the South Asian community. Dropping his last name meant that he was losing a part of his identity. He justi-fied his decision by telling himself that maybe one day, when he became legal, he could keep his real last name too. That desire fueled his fire to believe in another day for the chance he'd been waiting for his whole life.

My father woke up one day, feeling like he had no purpose. He was trying to do whatever he could to have anyone sponsor him to get a green card, but he always came up short. He turned to listen to the radio he had in his room. Every morning, he would wake up and hear the news and listen to some American pop music to start his day. That day, he heard on the radio that there was a town in California that needed farmers. The farm was offering sponsorship for a green card if the farmer worked with them for nine months.

Pinching himself to make sure he wasn't dreaming, my father smiled from ear to ear. He came from a long line of farmers and landowners back home in Punjab. That very day, he told his employer that he was moving to California for work. He packed whatever belongings he had and told his brother he was on his way to becoming an American citizen.

For the next nine months, he worked day and night to make sure the farming company could give him a green card. When your dream is within your grasp, you morph yourself into a superhuman who is unable to do anything else but obtain that dream. My father worked almost *every* hour he was awake; he was patiently moving toward his dream.

Finally, after a tireless pursuit, my father had his green card in his hands. Being validated with a green card made him feel like he was moving in the right direction. He immediately went back to New York to tell his brother what he was going to do next: leave for India to marry his fiancé and see the family that he left two years ago. The green card gave him permission to leave and come back to America. Legally. One of the first privileges he experienced as an American.

MASTERING BUTTERFLIES

ON DECEMBER 6, 1987, MY MOTHER AND FATHER GOT MARried. My father stayed in India for twenty days before he had to return to the States. Leaving his wife behind again was difficult; my father felt heartbroken because there was no official way that he could bring her to America. In typical arranged marriages, you meet the person you are marrying weeks before the wedding or even on the day of the actual ceremony. Having a three-year-long engagement is extremely unusual. The bond they created during those three years and the upheavals they faced (together but separately in two different countries) shaped the foundation of their love. Imagine getting engaged/married and leaving the person you love behind without any certainty of when or if you will see them again. The love sacrifices that South Asian parents experience in their immigration stories are often silenced because they want to be modest.

Since my father wasn't a full American citizen yet, he felt incomplete. The immigration process is long and tiresome. If you're illegal, you must find sponsorship for a green card. Once you have your green card, you must legally live in the States for five years before you can apply for citizenship. Only then are you considered a full American citizen. My father longed for that day. Being a citizen came with a lot of privileges, but the one privilege he wished he had immediately was to sponsor his wife to come to America. Even though he could now lawfully *stay* in America, he couldn't bring the woman he loved back to his new home.

My mother started looking for solutions and settled on one: she could visit my father on a visitor visa until he was naturalized. My mother was able to get a visitor visa easily because she had a master's in English. She indicated she was going to America for the holidays. After waiting for a month and providing all the necessary paperwork for a visitor visa, she received the green light to travel. My father and mother both decided they could think through how to bring her over legally after my father was an official citizen, but for now, they just wanted to be together—for as long as they possibly could.

Before boarding her flight to America, my mother started dreaming about what freedom would look like. *Could women be whatever they wanted? Were they able to do whatever their hearts desired?*

She made up her mind that once she was a citizen, she wanted to further her education and become a lawyer. Throughout the twenty-one-hour flight, she experienced a lot of emotions, but the one that occupied most of her heart was panic. She knew nobody in America, except for her husband. The thought of being alone terrified and excited her at the same time. When she finally landed, she was overwhelmed by anxiety; she didn't know what to do. Since this was the era before cell phones, my father had told her to wear a pink salwar kameez. He promised he would be holding a pink balloon and wearing a pink shirt so that she could spot him easily. She was traveling light—only one suitcase and enough money to get to her destination and back. As soon as she cleared customs, she searched everywhere for him but couldn't find him. Her heart sank, and she started to get nervous. *Where is he? What if I can't find him? Where would I go?* She did the only thing she knew how to do; she turned to Waheguru.

Waheguru, please give me strength. I'm really scared.

Just then, she saw my father's smiling face in the crowd and started to run toward him.

Mother: *I'm here! I'm here! I'M HERE, JI.*

Father: *I'm so glad you are here. Welcome to America.*

Smitten by his smile, my mother fell more deeply in love with him.

They drove home in a borrowed car that my father used for work, the iconic New York City taxi. My father told her to freshen up, so he could take her to her next surprise—downtown New York. She quickly got dressed so she could go out and see what New York looked like. It was like nothing she imagined. She looked around and felt like she was in a different world. Everywhere she looked, she was introduced to something new: buildings as tall as the sky, streetlights hitting her eyes like different spectrums of a rainbow, different types of people—rich in diversity like a rainforest. The sound of people speaking languages she couldn't understand all blended together in perfect harmony like a thunderstorm. Foods that her nose couldn't recognize but sparked curiosity in her taste buds. She heard the rush of nonstop work as they drove past Times Square, Fifth Avenue, and Wall Street and over the bridges and through the tunnels that connected the boroughs of New York City, the land of the free. She sighed and took a deep breath—to feel freedom.

Part III

———

FORGING
THE DREAM

MARTYR OF LOVE

MY MOTHER'S FIRST FEW WEEKS IN AMERICA WERE A breath of fresh air. She felt free and felt like she could be anything. My father would take her to see the new friends he made while working. Visiting them made her feel like a piece of home was here. She started making friends with their wives and dreaming about becoming a lawyer after she had her papers. She felt like she had a chance. She was naturally inquisitive and always asked questions to figure out how she could apply for legal residence. She was determined to find a way.

Figuring out how to navigate the different sidewalks of New York was like figuring out how to walk again. My parents were learning how to live a life here that was drastically different from their life in Punjab. As any new couple learning about themselves after they were married, they would take comfort in eating foods around town. They would try any Indian restaurant they could find because they missed being back home. After every adventurous meal they could afford, they took the long way home as an excuse to walk and see if there were any new ice cream places they could try. My mother loved ice cream, and my father knew it. After every workday, he would make time to get her ice cream. While he worked, mom was learning how to assimilate to America and the family she was living with. Every day was full of hope. They laughed, explored, and learned what it meant to live together and be each other's only support system. America was teaching them how to love each other more, and for that, they were grateful.

Indian parents never talk to their children about reproductive health, even after they are married. It wasn't long before my mom arrived in America that she realized she was pregnant with me. A million thoughts went through her head...

I can't stay here! I must go back! But I'm pregnant in America with an American baby, right? What about my dreams? I want to study! I want to become something! I want to help my husband. I want to make sure I can provide for my family back home in India. But now I'm going to be a mother?

My mother was going through an internal conflict and didn't know what to do. She knew she was here temporarily, but she also knew that she was technically carrying an American baby if he/she could be born here. Here was her chance to take the biggest risk of her life—to stay in America illegally, to deliver me.

When she told my father the news, he was pleasantly surprised. He was thrilled that there was going to be a little baby soon. Not any baby, but his own. He took it upon himself to figure out the safest things for his wife to eat while she was pregnant. Indian people are the most superstitious people on the planet. If you sneeze while you're leaving, you must go back into the house, take off your shoes, eat a piece of Gur (sugar), and then you can leave again. If you're pregnant, the superstitions are endless. My father would feed my mother all types of fruits to make sure she and the baby were happy and healthy. There are certain fruits that you should eat to make sure you have a boy, and my mom ate those too.

Being on a visitor visa meant my mother didn't have health insurance. In the beginning of her pregnancy, the only prenatal care I received was whatever food she ate. My mother didn't go to monthly doctor appointments. Luckily, she didn't receive a sonogram confirming my gender either.

I know what you're thinking: *Your mother is educated; she should know better. She should have figured out how to get some sort of prenatal care.* It is dangerous not receiving any. But the truth is that life is all about trade-offs. The trade-off she faced was being deported or staying without prenatal care at the chance of providing her unborn child a future here. She chose the latter, even if it meant that she and the baby could experience complications during her pregnancy.

I can't imagine what my life would have been like if I were born in India, but what amazes me the most is the immigrant fear of backtracking. Backtracking is a fear every immigrant family recognizes. It's a feeling that you *must* push ahead and never look back, no matter how hard or difficult things might seem. That same fear kept my mother in America and let me become an American citizen.

RELUCTANT EMBRACE

MY MOTHER WAS DETERMINED TO FIGURE OUT A WAY TO get health insurance for her and her unborn baby. A few months into her pregnancy, she learned about NYC's Medicaid and CHIP program—the Child Health Insurance Program. Immigrants in New York are offered more health insurance options than in any other state in America. There are six programs that New York offers immigrant mothers. My mother qualified for the Child Health Plus plan that offers health insurance regardless of her immigration status or income. This need-based program gave my parents a sense of security. America's generosity was bigger than their imagination. The American health care system cared about their growing family even if my mother didn't know if she could stay here after she gave birth to me.

The immigrant experience is hard. My parents often felt insignificant and vulnerable. Being in a new environment, among a new culture, while trying to figure out your new journey is overwhelming. As an illegal immigrant, you feel invisible in America, on a constant dog chase trying to "make it." Being a green card holder made my father feel like he was in an endless purgatory with no end in sight. He desperately wanted to make it to heaven: US citizenship.

My father felt doubt and vulnerability creeping into his mind as he started thinking about how he was going to afford to feed three mouths on his current salary as a taxi driver. His was the only income in his family. *What if something happens to me?* His anxiety of not being enough for his growing family arose every single day of his wife's pregnancy.

He was able to confine and find comfort on one thought. That thought being that his future child had won the lottery ticket he'd been desperately working toward—receiving a Social Security number the minute they took their first breath.

Progress.

THREE DEADLY WORDS: "IT'S A GIRL."

AS A WOMAN THINKING ABOUT HAVING CHILDREN SOON, I reached out to my mother to ask about her birthing experience in America.

What insurance did you have? When did you start taking prenatal? Did you and Papa talk about the right time to have kids? Were you scared to be a mom?

When I asked all these questions, I realized my mother was having a hard time understanding me.

What do you mean by insurance? We only had one option—the grateful program in NYC for mothers like me. Prenatal care? I didn't even know I was pregnant!

However, she did understand my anxiety.

I was absolutely terrified to be a mom; I didn't even know who I was, and your father and I were trying to figure out what to do in America.

I was a Medicaid baby. I was born in Queens General Hospital, one of the biggest public benefit corporation hospitals in the States. My mother was in labor for over forty-eight hours before she gave birth to me naturally. When she reminisces about the day I was born, she mentions how scared she was. How she didn't have her mother there to console her. How she didn't have anyone to turn to, to ask questions about what she was going to experience as a woman. Thinking about giving birth one day without my mother gives me anxiety—but my mother, she pushed through her anxiety *alone* and came out *fearless*. When I was born, my gender was revealed, along with expectations of what I could and could not become. Being born a girl is hard. Being born an Indian girl is a little harder. Being born the eldest daughter to a first-generation Indian American household is punishment. Is there a reset button?

My father was upset that I was born a girl. He was happy to have a child, but he had prayed that they would receive a son first. Even though he wasn't happy about my gender, there was one reality he couldn't escape: I was here, and he had to take care of me. My mother loved me the minute I came out. When the doctors told her, "Congratulations, it's a girl," she smiled and said, "My new best friend!" Within minutes of my arrival, I was laughing, giggling, and trying to absorb my surroundings. The doctors were surprised how active I was as a newborn. But there weren't any congratulatory balloons. This wasn't a celebration; it was a mourning.

When we went home, people visited my parents, congratulated them, and wished them well, but eventually, everyone went home, and we had to carry on. The pictures of our Gurus came down because I was born a girl. My mother held me close; she was upset this was happening. She pleaded with Waheguru to protect me, to give my little body strength, for me to grow up and be the most outspoken woman in the world.

People can't treat you this way just because you are a girl. You are my girl, the best girl, the only girl I will ever need. Don't give up, Sabi.

Now, I can't recall my experiences as a newborn, but I do remember the first time I was told that my gender made my father upset. I know what you're thinking.

Your dad is mean! How could he think and act that way!

I was mad about that for a good portion of my life too. But life has taught me to give someone you love the opportunity to grow. I knew my father loved me from the minute I was born. He just didn't understand *how* to love me yet.

Slowly, my father noticed how I looked like him, and he started to smile. He couldn't get over how tiny I was, so he put me in a small cabinet and took a picture of me because I looked like a perfect little doll. He would play with me and put me on his tummy. He would tickle my face with his beard and giggled when he saw me cry because it irritated me. We would work out together in the living room. He would lift his dumbbells, and I would kick my feet quick and fast like babies do. I grew up feeling that love—every single day.

News had spread to both my parent's families in India that they just had a daughter. Their reaction to my birth in India was different than in America; it was joyous and delightful. My Dadaji (dad's father) requested that they send him a picture of his new granddaughter as soon as possible, so he could keep it in his pocket always because she was a piece of his heart. My Nana and Nani (mother's father and mother) were floored by my arrival; they called me Kaur Junior.

I grew up wondering why the news of my birth was so joyous in India. In the Indian culture, daughters are a burden—shouldn't the news have made them sad? The truth is that daughters are more expensive than sons, and my birth was celebrated in India because they did not have any monetary obligations to raise me. To an Indian immigrant father in America, having a daughter was a setback when all he was trying to do was provide a foundation for his family. His daughter needed money and protection; this is what his culture told him and, regardless of where you live in the world, culture follows you.

To make matters worse, my father knew that a daughter would eventually leave him behind because it is her destiny to be married off into another family. He was preparing himself to let me go from the minute I was born. He knew I would leave his family. It doesn't matter what foundation he could provide or how happy he could make my life. Indian daughters always leave. That is our culture.

CAMOUFLAGED "CITIZEN"

LIKE MANY NEW PARENTS, MY PARENTS WERE STILL FIGuring out my first name. But they had already decided that my last name would be Kang—the name my father left behind when he left his country.

When the nurse came with the naming paperwork, they asked if my parents had decided on my first name. My parents said they needed more time, but they knew my nickname—Sabi (which means young girl). Somehow the paperwork got finalized, and they signed the birth certificate with my name as Sabi Kaur Singh. My parents lost it and asked if they could correct my name immediately. They were still thinking about my first name, but my last name was completely wrong. It wasn't Singh; it was Kang. My mother recalls her experience vividly.

They assumed that your last name was Singh because that is your father's name on his papers but that is not really his last name! I had to argue with the lady. I said that in my culture, when people come to America, they drop their last name and adapt Singh because everyone knows that a Singh or Kaur is from our religion. But our family given name is Kang. It always will be Kang and she is a Kang. Please fix her name immediately.

The lady who was completing the naming paperwork was incredibly annoyed. She worked with people like my mother all day, and they were all the same—illiterate and submissive. This Indian woman aggravated her because she knew some English and felt like she could challenge the way she did her work. She didn't understand why she was making a big fuss. She filled out the paperwork according to what everyone else does after their child is born: take the father's last name as the child's last name and use the mother's last name as the child's middle name. She didn't care if my mother was upset. She told her that she had already sent in the papers and that my mother could fix my name after the certificate came in the mail. The state sends you a draft to check for errors; if there are errors, you can correct them and send it back to the Department of Health in New York City.

My mother was using the only ID she had (her Indian passport) to correct her, and that seemed to further irritate the nurse. My mother tried to explain to her what happened.

My husband is stupid; his family couldn't get him to honor his family name on his ID, and he chose whatever name he wanted! He's crazy! Don't look at his last name. I'm telling you the truth that the correct family name is Kang. You must believe me. Even if it's not on our documents.

The nurse told my mother that she had done her job, and if my mother had an issue, she could correct it when the official paperwork came in the mail. Crushed but determined to correct what happened, my mother closed her eyes to focus on the only thing that could get her out of there: resting.

After my mother was discharged, she waited every day for the birth certificate to come in the mail. Once she finally received it, she corrected my name and sent back the paperwork.

Letting out a sigh of relief, my mother felt like her first decision as a new parent was corrected. My mother made sure that my father's family identity was given to me correctly. Imagine a 1990s America where your mother and father's last names are different from the last name given to you on your birth certificate. I was the first citizen in our family. I had to start my life with the correct name so our family could finally be visible. After my mother had me, she decided to stay in America. She didn't know what would happen or how hard the immigration process would be; all she knew was that she couldn't leave me behind to follow the societal rule of what you are supposed to do to become a citizen. She was a mother first and protecting me became her fate—even if it meant she was risking her ability to obtain legal citizenship.

Even now, I am amazed at how outspoken my mother was as an undocumented woman of color. She wasn't afraid to speak her mind and challenge the nurse because she felt that she was protected in America. She discovered her voice, for the first time, regardless of what her immigration status was. She believed that the laws in America protected her, even if she was undocumented. She was afraid to speak up in India, but America was a new starting point. A place that made her discover that she *had* a voice. That confidence made her feel American, even if she wasn't an American yet. It is because of that growing confidence that she spoke up for me and my family time and time again. Her voice shaped our destiny in America, even if it couldn't shape her cultural confidence in herself as an Indian woman.

SILENCING THE UNSPOKEN TRUTH

MY FATHER WAS WORKING DAY AND NIGHT TO MAKE MORE money, and my mother was spending all her waking hours taking care of me and still trying to maintain her own sanity. I was around five months old when my mother discovered that she was pregnant again.

Back at the flat my father shared with his brother, things were starting to get a bit crowded. It wasn't long after I was born that my parents started to feel like their presence was no longer welcome. My father's brother and sister-in-law had three kids of their own, my parents were living with them, and now, there was a new baby in that same apartment. When it comes to living with your extended family, drama is inevitable. There would be fights and disagreements; my parents felt on edge. Things started to get worse when our extended family realized my mother was pregnant again. That would mean *another* child in the tiny, cramped apartment. The arguments and fights would get so bad that my mother and father would start fighting with each other. How could you even blame them? How can any marriage survive so many hardships? They were children themselves, raising children, without help, learning what to do in America while constantly worrying about their next paycheck.

Even though every pregnancy is different, my parents felt more prepared for their second one. My father continued to do what he did best: bring home healthy food for everyone to eat. Even on his darkest and hardest days, he gave his all to his wife. Since it was her second pregnancy, my mother was more aware of what she should do. She also had health insurance this time and felt more comfortable being healthy for herself and her unborn baby.

When my mother talks about her second pregnancy, she mentions how it was easier, happier, and felt like it was shorter than her first one. I wondered to myself: *Why?*

Something seemed off, so I dug deeper into her silence. I started to ask questions that I hoped would answer the void I felt as a child growing up.

Why was she happier with her second pregnancy? Did she not love carrying me and being with me as a baby? How can this unborn baby provide her with more happiness than me? I was physically here. Was I not enough?

The only logical reason I could think of was that she knew she was having a boy but never told anyone.

As an adult, I became suspicious and suspected my theory was correct. It was burning a hole in my heart.

Why aren't there any pictures of our sonograms? Did mom not know the gender of her babies until we were born? I thought people could get sonograms in the 90s. Or are sonograms a modern technological thing?

I researched when sonogram machines were created and when hospitals adopted them, and I learned that sonograms had been around in America since 1950. I approached my mother to get clarity and found her evasive.

Me: *Mom, did you get a sonogram when you were pregnant with me and my brother?*

Mom: *No! I didn't want to hurt the baby, you know.*

Me: *No, Mom, it doesn't hurt the baby. Did you get one?*

Mom: *No! I didn't. Why would I put something inside of myself?*

Me: *No, Mom, they don't put anything inside of you, they usually put a gel on your stomach and do an ultrasound.*

Mom: *Leave me alone, Sabi; I'm busy.*

Me: *Mom, did you get a sonogram? Please tell me.*

Mom: *I already told you, "No." You know in India, it's now illegal to get a sonogram.*

I sensed she was distracting me because I was getting closer to the truth.

Me: *Mom, I'm asking about your sonogram.*

Mom: *They don't let people get one because they abort girls, you know. America is different, thank god. But India made it illegal to have a sonogram now, so they are learning too.*

Me: *MOM! I'm asking if you got one here.*

Mom: *Sabi, LEAVE ME ALONE.*

Now, I don't know for sure if my mother got a sonogram or

not, but her reaction makes me wonder if she knew the gender of both of her children. If she did, she withheld the truth from everyone, including her husband. She was afraid of the Indian culture and what that would mean for her firstborn child. I'm assuming she withheld the truth the second time around because she didn't want anyone to know about the first time. Being afraid to speak up and tell the truth is an experience every single South Asian woman knows. Our culture teaches us silence. *Be quiet. Obey. Don't resist. Do what you're told.* If my assumption is correct, my mother is still holding on to her silence today. Silence can take over your whole life if you let it.

The more I thought about it, the more sense it made to me. It would explain why my parents had such polarizing reactions to my birth. My father was shocked because it was the first time he realized that he was going to raise a daughter. My mother learned about my gender alone, and by the time I was born, she had made her peace with the responsibility of raising a daughter. The societal and cultural expectations of raising South Asian daughters are hard to face. Indian women are forced to have sex-selection abortions. The reason South Asian women stay silent is because this practice is still common today. Instead of having the uncomfortable conversation to address the truth, immigrant mothers confine themselves to the only hope they have to maintain a peaceful house: remain voiceless and silence their deepest secrets.

INCONSPICUOUS DUTY

MY FATHER RECEIVED A PHONE CALL THAT EVERY CHILD fears—his father had suddenly passed away at the age of fifty-eight. His family wanted him to come back to India to perform the final burial rituals. Shocked, hurt, confused, and in complete disbelief, he collected all the money he could get to board a redeye to India.

Funerals hurt. They hurt a little more if the person you desperately wanted to show your "American success" to is gone. Being the youngest, my father was a mischievous boy growing up. His childhood was full of disobedience and doing whatever his heart desired. When he left for America, he was determined to show his father that he could reform into a respectful, responsible, and resourceful son. He yearned for his father's approval. He never thought in his wildest dreams that his father was going to die before he could see him become a proper man. His father was never going to see what he could become.

Burying his father shocked his soul. His mind was racing.

What's the point? It feels like God is always after me. Everything is more difficult than it needs to be. I'm a father to a baby girl in America, and in the same year, my own father is gone? What did I do in my last life to deserve this?

After the cremation, he learned that his father was cremated in the clothes and the wallet he always kept with him. In that wallet was the last piece of mail he would ever send his father: a picture of his daughter, Sabreet. He took a deep breath as his fear encompassed him. It was during the wake of his father's death that he realized he no longer had to show his father he was grown up; he was already grown. His responsibilities not only increased the day his daughter was born, but they also increased the day his father died. He and his brother were now fathers to their three sisters in India. The night before he left, he couldn't recognize the man he saw in the mirror. He felt and looked different but couldn't understand why.

His flight back to America was hard. The last time he had seen his family was for his wedding. The next time he met them was for a funeral. Life changes so quickly sometimes that there is no time to process what just happened. It was responsibility after responsibility. He thought about his father's alcoholism and couldn't help but wonder if his drinking contributed to his sudden death. One harsh decision can impact your family in profound ways. Family is a collection of individual choices colliding together, forming a foundation of love and responsibility. There was one thing he knew for sure—his child deserved the best of him. The feeling he felt right now, no child should experience that. Feeling without purpose. Empty. Like nothing mattered. He vowed to devote all his time to his daughter and unborn child. I was all he had, and now I was the reason he wanted to be respectful, responsible, and resourceful. As soon as he landed, he watched me let go of my welcome back balloon and scream, "Papa!"

Part IV

———

SEARCHING FOR SELF AND COMMUNITY

EXILED

ONE DAY IN 1993, MY PARENTS CAME HOME TO LEARN THAT the house they shared with their extended family was no longer a viable place to live. The furniture was gone, and all the utilities in the apartment had been disconnected. There was no note from my father's brother; they had disappeared as if they had gotten abducted. The only thing that remained was the mattress that my parents, my brother, and I slept on. The message was loud and clear.

You are on your own.

That day, my parents experienced a sinking feeling they couldn't describe. Their reality had completely changed. They were homeless in America and had nowhere else to go. They didn't know who to turn to. My father thought about calling his brother-in-law who lived in Wisconsin, but he didn't want to worry him. There was no way he could move his entire family across the country. They couldn't stay in the apartment because there was no heat or running water. They didn't know how long they had until the landlord showed up. They knew nothing. All they knew was they had to leave immediately with no destination in mind.

Earlier that year, my mom had become associates with another Indian woman because they were both pregnant at the same time. My father knew her husband and had introduced them to each other, so they wouldn't be lonely as they embraced motherhood. During her time of need, my mother did the only logical thing she knew: she picked up the phone and called the only local friend that she had in New York. She told her what happened and asked if her family could stay with her for the night. The woman agreed. Overcome, my mother started to cry. She thanked Waheguru that a stranger was kind enough to give her family shelter for the night. We drove over in my father's taxi to her apartment. We returned to our old apartment in the morning to pick up what little belongings we had left behind.

My parents realized, as they tried to sleep that night, that they couldn't depend on anyone. To immigrate alone means you have no network—no friends or family you can depend on. You have nothing except the kindness of strangers. Strangers who might believe in giving you a shot and think you deserve common human decency. With two toddlers and no place to stay, my parents were reminded that all we had in America was each other.

Where would we have gone if that woman had said, "No"? Would my parents have gone to the homeless shelter in Queens? How could they? My father had a green card, and my mother was still getting her residency papers in order. What would have happened if we went to a homeless shelter? Would they have been detained and deported back even if their children were American citizens? Would they have been separated from their children and considered unwanted members of American society? The truth is my family wouldn't have a chance to survive in modern-day America. They survived back then because times were different. Maybe for the better.

Being homeless takes a toll on your mental health. My brother and I were too young to remember what happened, but we hear the vulnerability and fear our parents felt that night by the way our parents tell the story to this day. The lights didn't turn on in the apartment. They couldn't get a hold of my uncle. They didn't know who to turn to for the night. When they prepared themselves to immigrate to America, my parents understood that the journey was going to be hard, but they didn't realize that it would cost them their mental well-being.

South Asians are a community-based group, whereas Americans are individualistic. If some unforeseen circumstance occurs, you can always reach out to your family or any South Asian community member you know to help you. But what if you haven't formed one yet? What happens when your whole community is a different country? What if the people who made you homeless *were* your own family? Where do you go then? How can you stop thinking about the worst-case scenario when the reason you have a place to sleep tonight is out of sheer luck?

Having a place to call home is a privilege that no American should take lightly. Having a temporary home, even if it's for the night, is something no immigrant has ever taken lightly either.

SELF-SACRIFICING

LIKE MOST RISK-AVERSE IMMIGRANTS, MY PARENTS WERE looking for a home where they felt their working-class lifestyle could be understood.

What is the working-class lifestyle, and why is it important to feel understood? I understand this lifestyle as a complete devotion to work—all types of work, no matter what, where, or when you need to work. Work comes before family. Family comes after work. Work is what drives you and kills you at the same time. Family is *why* you work. Providing for them is your duty, but the driving force of your life is work. So, when my parents were looking for a new apartment complex for our family, they were looking at different working-class apartment complexes that could understand who they were and what their lifestyle needs were. They were looking for a community that could help them when they needed to work at any time. A hard-working melting pot—a working-class community that they could trust.

One of my father's taxi driver friends was living in an apartment complex that fit what my parents were looking for, and he told him there was a vacancy. My father was immediately interested and wanted to book the opening quickly. He reached out to the landlord and was able to finalize the paperwork for the lease within a day. About a week after we became homeless, my family had our own home. My parents had mixed emotions—grateful that my mother's friend let us stay through the week, sad that our time with her was ending, and fortunate that our family had a place of our own for the first time in America. We were moving to 144-47 Thirty-eighth Ave., Apt. #8, Flushing, NY 11354—a one-bedroom studio apartment that was 550 square feet with a monthly rent of $950.

Like every new experience, moving into a new apartment was a rush of emotion. The emotion that my parents felt the most was peace. They were at peace that they had a roof over their heads. As the days and weeks progressed, my parents started to form close relationships with their neighbors. These people became their safety net. If my mom needed a ride to the pediatrician because dad had to work, our next-door neighbor would take us. If mom went out to get groceries, I could run downstairs and open a family friend's apartment door (also known as "Auntie" or "Uncle" in the South Asian community) and ask for food if I was hungry. The doors in the apartment complex were always unlocked and always open. Everyone trusted each other, and help was always there, no matter what. It was the first time my parents felt as if they had finally found their people in America.

A few weeks went by in our new home, and my father decided that it would be best if my mother could be a stay-at-home mom and take care of us. He had been thinking about this for a while but ultimately landed on two reasons why staying at home was ideal: she could figure out how to adjust to America and get her green card at home (the safest option for her), and she would be able to protect and guide the children because we were our parents' investment plan.

My mother agreed to my father's decision and started to adjust to her new normal. The first thing my mom did was figure out how to get her green card. Now that she had two American-born children, she applied to get a green card through the family eligibility category, and her paperwork was processed quickly. Her next step was waiting five years before she could apply for citizenship. My mother wanted to help financially, so she started to make hair clips at home and sell them to people she knew in the apartment complex. My mother slowly realized the dreams she had for herself must be put on hold. She chose to erase the ambition she had before she had children. She didn't have time to become a lawyer. She didn't have time for herself anymore. She wanted to give herself fully and only to her family. They were her purpose now. Her only desire was to help them be whoever they wanted to be. In that dream, she hoped that maybe one day they could accomplish her dreams too. Sacrificing your dreams is a reality of every single immigrant parent. Sacrificing your identity and who you want to be because your faith in your children is so strong that you believe everything will be okay. This sacrifice has helped America build its future, time and time again.

GROWING CONFIDENCE

GROWING UP IN AN IMMIGRANT COMMUNITY IS A UNIQUE EXPE-
rience. Parents don't realize that their children remember
everything. When I was three years old, my love for ice cream
grew furiously. I would beg my father as soon as he would come
home from work to get me some ice cream. Smiling, he would say,
"Yes," and reminisce about his earlier ice cream experiences with
my mother. Even though I could sometimes sense that he was
sad because he was missing out on taxi fares, he never said, "No."

One day, my father was walking my brother and me down
the street after his taxi shift. My brother was in a stroller and I
was holding his hand, walking fearlessly down the block. Suddenly, I saw an ice cream truck and let go of my father's hand
in a millisecond. Without thinking, I started running across a
two-way street with oncoming traffic. Struck by fear, my father
started running after me.

Sabi! Sabi! No! Stop. Come here, please!

He looked to the left, where there was a school bus coming
in my direction at full speed. Immediately throwing his hands

up, he ran into the street in front of me, trying to stop the bus. By some miracle, the bus stopped, and my father grabbed me. With a small smile and tears in his eyes, my father lifted me up and told me that ice cream was canceled today. I cried, unaware of what had happened and upset that I would not be getting my dessert.

Ever since he came home from the funeral in India, my father started developing a deeper bond with me. I was his best friend. As soon as I was able to hold a conversation, I would ask him questions about the world. Whatever I learned from him, I would use to help answer the questions my brother had too. I ended every story by asking, "Hana ni, Papa?" which meant, "Do you agree with me, Dad?" Every single time I asked that question, his world would freeze, and he would answer "Hanji beta." (YYes, my child").

That confidence my father gave me helped me grow; it became a part of my childhood identity. Growing up, I wasn't your average-sized girl. Being in a Punjabi household, my parents believed in whole milk and butter because they made our bones strong. When I was around four years old, I was playing tag with my brother in my apartment. Being close in age, my brother and I were best friends. We would play with each other's toys. There was only one problem: he would run over my Barbies with his truck, and it would infuriate me. It got so bad one day that I got up and started running around the coffee table to chase him. I chased him around and around and around—for what felt like a thousand rounds. I kept going. I was determined to catch him. Faster, stronger, quicker, with my eyes locked on catching him by the shoulder. I kept chasing him for what felt like forever, and in a split second, he made a right turn toward the TV. I ran to grab him, but I missed and ran right through our locked glass balcony door that led to the patio in our apartment. I ran right through the door, and I managed to not get a scratch on me. Panicking, my mother came over to yell at me and check to see if I was alright. I got in a lot of trouble, but I remember feeling like a superhero that day. A superhero that got her powers by drinking whole milk.

Even though we were growing up feeling confident, our parents didn't always feel that way. Even at the youngest of ages, children can be a light for their parents. Nothing scared my mother more than driving a car. She couldn't wrap her head around how people in America drive, especially in New York City. The roads had more order here than in India, but it was still scary. Everyone drives so fast—faster than a New York minute. Before she could try, she convinced herself that she was never going to be capable of driving, until my four-year-old brother came along. Innocently playing with his toy car, he asked mom one day...

Brother: *Mummy, why don't you drive cars?*

Mom: *Jaan, I don't know how.*

Brother: *Why?*

Mom: *I don't need to drive. We have the subway.*

Brother: *But, Mummy, I don't want a mummy that doesn't know how to drive. How will you drive a sports car then?*

Mom: *Don't be silly.*

Brother: *Mummy, you need to learn how to drive. I know you can do it; don't be scared. Please, Jaan doesn't ask for anything. Can you please learn how to drive, so we can drive together in a car one day?*

Mom: *Jaan, it's not important right now.*

Brother: *But, Mummy, it is! I need to have a mom that knows how to drive a car. Promise me you will learn to drive a car. For Jaan?*

Mom: *Okay, Jaan, I promise I will try.*

My mother didn't take him seriously and thought he would forget, but my brother was persistent. He followed up with her every day. *When was she going to go take the test?* Finally, she caved, so he would stop asking her every day. She said she would get her driver's license if he agreed to one condition—she wouldn't drive in New York. He agreed instantly. He was excited to have a mother who could drive. He didn't care if she didn't drive in real life; he only cared about the fantasy he had about them driving together in a sports car one day.

The beauty of having a close-knit family is that we are all we need and all we have is each other. Building courage and strength in each other is a two-way street. Whenever we were scared to dream, our parents protected our innocence and reminded us that we were living in a land full of promise and opportunities. All we had to do was believe we could become anything we wanted. If we believed it hard enough, we could become exactly that. When our parents couldn't show that same kindness to themselves, we told them the only thing they had to fear was thinking they aren't enough. If they ever lacked any confidence, all they had to do was look at the confidence we, their children, were growing each day. In our innocent ways, we continuously reminded each other what love and courage can help us do. Family doesn't have to be complex—it can be simple. To us, family meant being there for each other, even in the greatest of insecurities.

KINDNESS

EVEN THOUGH I GREW UP HERE, THE FIRST LANGUAGE taught to me was Punjabi. My parents decided that they were not going to teach us English at home. If they spoke to us in English, we would never learn Punjabi, and our native language would be lost. There would be plenty of opportunities to learn English, but learning Punjabi was rare. I grew up learning Punjabi and picked up some English through television.

We learned everything we could through television. It was magical. There were Indian channels that showed us what was happening in India. We obsessed and grew to appreciate the importance of the different channels we watched. Nothing brought us a greater sense of appreciation than watching something together. The television essentially shaped what school I went to in New York.

My mother spent all her time trying to research and learn about the education system in America, so she could set us up for success. In the 1990s, conducting research involved physical work. My mother would visit the library and different public service facilities to get answers to the questions she had. She had one stroller and two children. She would hold one of us on her hip and place the other in the stroller as she made her rounds around town, trying to piece together information. She did her best to learn whatever she could. She sought out information that would tell her what to teach us, which districts had the best public schools in Queens, and everything else in between.

After learning about the school district disparities in Queens, she became worried about the district I was assigned to for kindergarten. District 32 was crowded, had fewer teachers, and had overall lower test scores than District 25. Because of where we lived, I could not go to the District 25 school. My mom was so afraid of setting me up for failure from the get-go, she even had me interviewing at different Catholic private schools that we couldn't afford. Even with my minimal English-speaking skills, I was accepted into several private Catholic schools. The tuition was outrageous, and the subway commute was impossible to get there. My mom felt hopeless and trapped because she couldn't see a way out of my District 32 destiny. Distraught, she turned to Waheguru at night for guidance.

One morning, she wasn't feeling herself. She woke up a bit later than usual and was brushing her teeth while listening to the CBS local news. She noticed that the superintendent for Queens was at a shop that was a ten-minute walk from our apartment. He was talking about his vision for schools in the future. Within fifty seconds, my mom was dressed in a salwar kameez and had pushed us out of the house—she said we were going to go see the man in charge of all the schools in Queens. We were confused but happy; we were going on a mini adventure! My brother and I were hoping we could get some donuts on the way back home. My mother arrived at the location of the news shoot and started speaking her mind to the superintendent.

Mom: *Excuse me, sir; can I please have a minute of your time?*

The superintendent ignored her.

Mom: *Sir, I ran eight blocks with my children to see you.*

No answer.

Mom: *Sir, please, this is for my children.*

No answer.

Mom: *SIR, we came from India so we could give our children the opportunities to go to the best schools in the world, but I know that the test scores and teachers are better in District 25 than in the district my children will be placed in because we don't live in a better community. Is there any way I can send my kids to District 25? They are American citizens!*

The superintendent turned his head.

Superintendent: *What's your name, ma'am?*

Mom: *Satnam Kaur. Here is my daughter; she is supposed to start kindergarten next year.*

The superintendent gave my mom with a puzzled look.

Superintendent: *Listen, your daughter will go to the school she is assigned to—*

Mom: *NO, but sir...*

Superintendent: *For at least one year.*

Mom: *I don't understand.*

Superintendent: *Halfway through the school year, call the District 25 school. Ask them if there are any vacancies open. If there are spots open, ask them to schedule an interview with the principal.*

He handed his business card to my mom.

Superintendent: *Tell him I sent you. He will interview your daughter to make sure she is up to the standards of that school—which I don't think will be a problem because your daughter has a great example.*

The superintendent started to smile.
Almost in tears, my mother was only able to say one thing.

Mom: *Thank you so much, sir. God bless you. Thank you.*

My mother took a deep breath and looked over at us. "So, who wants donuts?" ME!

Halfway into my first year of kindergarten, my mother took me to interview with a principal at District 25. I remember feeling like I was in trouble because I was talking to a principal in a different district. She brought my brother along (who was dressed in a suit) and dressed me up in a fancy little dress. On our commute, mom was preparing me with potential questions he might ask. I don't remember how the interview went, but I remember that my brother would also answer the questions the principal was asking me after I was done speaking because we were both rehearsing on the subway. The principal smiled and noticed my clever brother. He indicated that next year both of us should come to District 25. Floored with excitement, my mom hugged us on our way out. She mentioned on our way home that the bus stop for this new school was down the street, right in front of the gurdwara. Walking out of that office was the first time my mother felt like she could make a difference in America with her children—by sending us to good schools.

When my mom told me this story as an adult, I became curious. As a researcher, I looked up the two different districts in Queens. When I looked up P.S. 184 in District 25, I was astonished by what I found. It was one of the top thirty public schools in New York. More than half of their students were minorities, had a great teacher-to-student ratio, and good overall test scores. I started thinking about what would have happened if I weren't given this opportunity by the superintendent. What if my mom wasn't watching the news late that morning? What if my mom didn't research school district differences for my brother and me? What would have happened to our educational career in New York? Behind every "what if" moment was an invisible force—kindness. The kindness of that superintendent changed the course of my life. The kindness of that District 25 principal gave my brother and me the opportunity to go to Public School 184. Going to the better district kept my family together because my mother couldn't arrange two separate bus stop drop-offs in the morning at the same time. A small act of kindness can change the course of someone's life. My brother and I are living proof of small acts of kindness, repeatedly, by complete strangers.

EDUCATIONAL ISOLATION

I BEGAN SCHOOL IN ESOL CLASSES, WHICH FELT LIKE A second home. All these kids understood me, and I understood them. The kids in my other classes made me feel different, and I couldn't understand why. I began to feel like I had to hide parts of who I was with different kids in my classes. I started to feel uncomfortable around kids who didn't look like me.

Even though I did all the homework assignments and paid attention in class, I always had *B*s or *C*s in reading and spelling the first few years I was in school. I didn't understand how the other kids knew how to read the words they didn't know. I thought they knew something I didn't. I was too shy to ask my teacher for help because I didn't want her to think I was different. I already felt different, and I didn't want the teacher to think differently of me. When my name was called to read out loud, I would freeze. I prayed that the teacher would move on, but she wouldn't, and I had to read. When I arrived at a word I didn't know, I would skip the word because who's listening anyway?

I was so uncomfortable with speaking English, I began to silence myself. If I didn't talk, how would anyone know I had a problem saying different words in English? Instead of growing confident, I grew shy. On all of my elementary school report cards, the message was clear.

Sabreet needs help with English and spelling.

My mother would fight for me the only way she knew how.

Please assign her more homework!

My reading comprehension worried her, so my mother thought of a new way to get help for me: assign me a pen-pal in India, my Nanaji. The more letters I wrote, the better I thought my writing was getting. The problem: in my letters, I was using the words I already knew. How could a child grow from using the same words they knew repeatedly? How was my mother supposed to know that I probably needed a tutor?

My parents had unwavering faith in the American school system. They believed everything was better here. There is some truth to that statement, I suppose. The air, the houses, the trees, and even the people are all nicer here. But regardless of where you end up in the world, you can never escape social stratification. America has an economic class system, and everyone has their rightful place in it. Regardless of your sacrifice or your struggle, you aren't guaranteed mobility to a higher economic class based on your merit. It's not that simple, and it's not that easy. Being a good person doesn't make you rich, and it doesn't mean your family will be provided for. Working hard doesn't guarantee you riches either. Just like attending a good public magnet school doesn't mean I would automatically become proficient in reading and writing English because I'm in America. The system doesn't work like that. Learning a new language doesn't work like that.

I hid behind my shyness and lack of ability because, even at my young age, I didn't have the courage to tell my mother that I was falling behind in school. If I voiced that I needed help, it would mean my parents' faith in the American system would be broken. As a child, I knew I had to keep quiet and pretend everything was okay. I had convinced myself that I would figure it out later. I would learn those skills later, maybe with a different teacher. I knew one thing for sure—that my battles with English were small in comparison to the battles my mother and father fought every day to provide for us. As a child, I convinced myself that I was all I had, and I had to fight my battles alone.

DEVELOPING A HYPHENATED EXISTENCE

I NEVER NOTICED RACE. MAYBE BECAUSE I LIVED IN NEW York and my neighbors were from all walks of life. Or maybe because I was truly ignorant to the fact that I was a fair-skinned brown girl. My skin color wasn't dark enough for people to fear me. The color of your skin shapes how people in society treat you.

As a child, my first understanding that people are different races was a bit puzzling. I came home from school one day upset because a couple of Caucasian kids on the bus were asking where I came from. I didn't know how to answer them. Upset, I started asking my mother questions.

Me: *Mom, what are we? Are we Indian? Am I not American?*

Mom looked at me with concern.

Mom: *Sabi, we are Indian. I told you, remember? We come from a village in Punjab called Khamano.*

Me: *But, Mom, there are kids who are just American in school. Why am I not like them?*

Mom: *What do you mean by "just American"? You are American. You were born here, and that makes you an American.*

Me: *So, I am two things? Indian and American? Am I an Indian American?*

Mom: *Yes! You can call yourself an Indian American if you like. You are Indian and American together, equally.*

Me: *Okay, I'll tell the kids in school that I'm an Indian American.*

Next day on the bus...

Me: *Hey! I asked my mom, and she said we are Indian Americans.*

White kid on the bus: *So, you're Native American? The ones that have feathers on their heads and who come to Thanksgiving?*

Me: *I don't know, but I know I'm Indian and American.*

White kid on the bus: *Oh, you're like from here. So, you're Native American Indian. Tell your mom when you get home because I think she's confused too.*

Me: *Okay.*

After school...

Me: *Mom, you didn't tell me we were also Native American Indians.*

Mom: *No, we are not Native Americans; we are Indians from India. Who is asking you all these questions? Your teacher? I will come to school and fix her.*

Me: *No, this kid on the bus.*

Mom: *Was he a boy?*

Me: *Yes.*

Mom: *Stay away from boys! They don't know what they are talking about, and you can't talk to boys. You can only be friends with girls. If a boy talks to you, you ignore them.*

Me: *Okay Mummy, I'm sorry.*

I never got to the bottom of what I was. I walked away from that conversation believing I was Indian, American, *and* Native American. Oh, and I learned I couldn't talk to boys.

By the time I was seven years old, I had learned that I didn't have an accent. I realized that people at school spoke English differently than everyone back at the apartment.

Asian boy: *Sabreet, your English is like all the white kids here.*

Me: *No, my English is like yours.*

Asian boy: *No! You're different. You speak like them.*

Me: *I do?*

Asian boy: *You're lucky.*

Silence.

I spoke English differently than the other kids who looked like me. *Why*? I realized that kid was right; people did have different accents when they spoke in English. I started to notice different English accents and then noticed that I have two accents. I had an Indian accent when I speak at home with my parents. I had a different accent when I spoke to my teachers in school. I tried to speak in a way where I felt like I could be understood. As a child, I had no idea that I had learned when it was appropriate to communicate with an Indian accent and when I shouldn't. I was mimicking the adults around me. Afraid of miscommunication, I learned how to communicate the same exact way as the people around me.

As a child of immigrants, you imitate everything. You imitate your parents, your classmates, and your teachers. You imitate everyone instead of trying to be yourself. My identity was confusing and nobody at school or home could tell me what I was. I grew up thinking that I was everything and everyone. I changed my behavior and what I believed in, according to the people I was around. At home, I was Indian. I spoke Punjabi, I believed in Waheguru, I ate North Indian food, and I didn't talk to boys—only my brother. At school, I spoke English. I ate cafeteria pizza. I talked to boys and girls because they were in my classes. I pretended I was American, even if I didn't feel like one. Americans have nothing to hide. I was hiding. I was living a double life where I was Indian at home and American at school. I continued to live these two different and distinct identities throughout my childhood. Being Indian and American, the constricting cultural values created confusion and mayhem in my heart. I felt like a misfit. An outsider looking into both the Indian and American cultures. I felt removed from my Indian identity and withdrawn from being American. I desperately wanted to fit in and be like all the American kids in classes; they seemed happy and proud to be who they were. They were normal.

One day in third grade, our teacher told us that we were having a beach day, the last day of school before summer break. We were supposed to bring in beach toys, dress in our bathing suits, and tell our parents to pack us beach snacks. I'd never been to the beach, so I was super excited. I ran home to tell my mom about beach day. I told her I needed a beach toy, a towel, and some snacks. Like every good mother, she made sure I had what I needed for the last day of school.

On the last day of school, I was thrilled to have my first beach experience. I woke up excited to go on the trip. After we recapped everything we learned and where we were going next year, it was time to relax. Our kindergarten teacher instructed everyone to get their beach supplies and change into their swimsuits.

I started panicking. I didn't have a swimsuit. I had enough common sense as a child to not ask my immigrant mother for a swimsuit. An Indian woman never shows her body—I had yet to see my own mother's legs! Even at this age, I knew better than to ask my mother for something that was never going to be allowed in my childhood. But, back in the classroom, everyone was getting ready in their swimsuits, and I didn't have the foresight as a child to think about what would happen at this exact moment. I didn't have a bathing suit to wear. I just had my normal clothes that I wore to school.

As I started to see what the kids were wearing as they entered the playpen, I realized I did have that. It looked like my underwear and the cami I was wearing under my clothes. Naïve, fearless, and carefree as could be, I took off my clothes and showed up at the playpen in my white-as-snow underwear and cami. I made sandcastles with the other kids, and nobody noticed that I was wearing my underwear. I felt like I got away with going to beach day without a swimsuit—until I didn't.

My teacher came over to me.

Teacher: *Sabreet, do you want a towel?*

Me: *No, I'm okay. I'm making another castle.*

Teacher: *I'm asking some of the kids to get dressed, so we can give other members in our class the opportunity to make sandcastles. Do you want to get dressed now and give your friends the chance to make some too?*

Me: *Okay, I can do that.*

I obeyed and left the playpen. I felt like I got in trouble. I thought maybe she knew I wasn't really wearing a swimsuit. I wasn't sure because I noticed that she was also asking the other kids to come out of the playpen. I remember feeling embarrassed that I had gotten caught but also confused because I wasn't entirely sure.

I'll never forget what happened when I went to give my teacher a hug at the end of the day. I told her I'd miss her, and I said, "Bye." She hugged me tight and said, "Always be brave, Sabreet." Maybe she did know? I'll never know. What I can tell you is this: I truly felt American that day by rejecting my Indian identity. My New York public school experience taught me how to be fearless, obedient, silent, respectful, and to persevere at the same time. That foundation shaped both of my identities, separately and equally.

THE RIGHT TO SURVIVE

THROUGHOUT THE NEXT SEVERAL YEARS, MY FAMILY started getting more comfortable about the life we were building in New York. My brother and I were getting used to going to school, dad was getting used to his tireless nights, and my mother finally felt like enough time had passed that she could get a job and help our family financially. After thinking about it for a while, my parents decided that we were old enough, so my mom could work.

There were a few things that they were still worried about. What would happen if one of them couldn't wake up in time to take us to the bus stop or come back in time to pick us up? Since my mother left home at three o'clock in the morning to work at Hudson News at the airport, she wouldn't be able to wake us up in time for the bus stop. My dad came home at two o'clock in the morning or later—giving him the responsibility to wake us up would be cruel. Together, my parents came up with a brilliant solution that would not only thrill us but also teach us responsibility—they told us it was our job to wake up in time to go to school.

All children want to feel like grown-ups as soon as they are born. Thrilled and excited, I tasked myself with the responsibility of waking up at 7:00 a.m. to get ready for school.

I would get ready first and then wake up my brother. Since we got free lunch at school, we didn't have to pack lunch, but I did have to figure out breakfast. I would usually eat toast or whatever mom would make before she left. After all the morning errands were done, there was one errand I couldn't do: I didn't know how to do my own hair. As an Indian girl, my mother braided my long, thick hair every morning before I went to school. Since my mom was working now, she obviously couldn't braid my hair, so my dad decided that he would learn how to do it. Our bus would come to the bus stop at 8:30 a.m.

As a child, my favorite part of our morning routine was trying to wake up my dad to braid my hair. I would start at 7:55 a.m. I would go into his bedroom and tap him lightly on his shoulder.

Me: *Papa, it's 7:55.*

Papa: *Okay, wake me up at 8:00.*

I would go back out to the living room and wait five more minutes.

Me: *Papa, it's 8:00. Can you do my braid?*

Papa: *Ten more minutes? Wake me up at 8:10.*

I would rush back out into the living room and wait ten minutes. Dad knew 8:10 was the last snooze because my brother and I would leave the house at 8:15 to get to our bus stop in time.

Me; (gently opening the bedroom door), *Papa, it's 8:10.*

Papa: *Okay, come here.*

Half asleep, he would sit up on his bed. I would sit on the floor and wait for him to do my braid. He would comb my hair and do my braid, but it always looked different than the ones my mom did. Sometimes, he was so sleepy he couldn't fully braid my hair neat and clean like my mother would, so I would use a butterfly clip to make it look prettier. After he was done braiding my hair each morning, he would say, "Okay, go to school…be careful."

My brother and I would walk one block away from our apartment to catch our bus. Having the gurdwara in front of our bus stop felt like a true blessing. Every new school year, any test, any problem we had, my brother and I would go to the bus stop early to Matha Tak (pray) before school. Those mornings became my most treasured memories of our independence as children in New York. After school, we would either go to the gurdwara or wait for my mom to come and get us. If she ever ran late, she would find someone she trusted to get us. After a while, we felt like we could do it all. Everything was going according to our plan—until it wasn't.

One afternoon, our schedule was thrown off. Mom wasn't around, and we didn't know what was going on. Someone from the apartment came and got us from the bus stop, and we waited at home. They told us that mom had some accident going to work and she needed to talk to the police. Scared of the unknown, we didn't know what to make of it and restlessly waited for our mom to come home to tell us what happened.

When Mom finally came home, she looked downcast and a little bruised around her arms and face.

Us: *Mom, what happened? We were so scared.*

Mom: *Nothing, just a bad guy was trying to steal my purse on my way to the subway this morning.*

Us: *What kind of bad guy? What was he trying to do?*

Mom: *He came from behind me and started to pull on my purse hard and started to hit me. He was trying to steal my money.*

My brother and I looked at each other in disbelief.

Us: *Mom, are you okay?*

Mom: *Don't worry, beta; I am fine. I kicked his ass. I kicked and kicked and hit him back and took my purse back, and quickly ran inside the station that was full of light.*

Us: *You kicked and hit the bad guy?*

Mom: *Yes! I wasn't going to let him think he could take whatever he wanted. I fought for what is mine. Nobody can come and take anything away from you if you fight back. Nobody, you hear me? It doesn't matter if you are a boy or girl. You fight always. We have worked too hard to let anyone come and take what we have worked so hard for. Don't let anyone ever take advantage of you.*

Us: *Okay, mom.*

Not only were we scared of the world now, but we were also aware that we had to fight back if someone tried to harm us. We didn't understand *why* someone would try to hurt us. We thought everyone lived honestly. What we did know from this day on was that bad guys do exist, even if it doesn't seem like they do. Mom was going to work, and someone attacked her. *Why would someone do that?* Mom was trying to make money for her family. She wasn't going to let that man take whatever little money she had in her purse because she worked way too hard for it. *You must fight and be alert, always.*

My whole world changed that day—America wasn't as safe as we thought. For the first time in my childhood, I became afraid of the world and everything around me. People hurt other people for money. *How could this be the land of the free if people hurt one another?* As children, we started to realize that there was a lot more to life than we knew.

FOREIGNER'S HOLY GRAIL

FEELING UNSEEN AND GIVING YOURSELF FULLY TO A COUNTRY you are still fighting to call your home is the reality of every immigrant brave enough to try to become American. Being an immigrant comes with a sense of invisibility. As an undocumented immigrant, your invisibility seems like a blessing. You don't want to get caught, so you stay hidden until you finally get a green card. Even if you are physically working every single minute to help the American economy, you pray for this invisibility to cloak you until you are a true citizen, five years later.

My father felt invisible while being my family's hero in the early 1990s. Not only was he a hero to the family he created, but he was also a hero to the family he left back in India. The problem was that he never *felt* like a hero. What he was doing felt small; no matter how hard he tried, he didn't feel good enough. He barely slept, worked tirelessly to provide for us, and he felt strangely empty. That feeling had started to fade a little after he received his green card. But it came back. Even though he was physically working, his mind was mentally torturing him for everything he couldn't become immediately. The invisibility my father had once prayed for now felt like a curse. After putting his blood, tears, and sweat into this country, it became a constant reminder of how insignificant he was to America.

I'm still not a citizen.

My father had a hard time understanding and controlling his thoughts of inferiority created because of his immigration status. Like every immigrant parent, my father persevered against all odds—the problem was he couldn't see the progress he was accomplishing. After five years of waiting, my father was finally able to apply and receive his citizenship. The day he had been waiting for—for what felt like his whole life. The irony of finally arriving at the threshold of your dreams is that you instantly lose why you cared about this dream in the first place. After receiving his citizenship, my father felt empty. He had imagined that he would experience a surreal moment after gaining citizenship to the greatest country in the world. But he didn't. He felt the same. The same person he was when he left his native country. He envisioned that he would be a richer, better-off man when he was a citizen. But nothing changed. He was still that poor man who left that ship; the only difference was that now he was a poor man with American citizenship.

After he passed his citizenship test, my father went back to work because he couldn't afford to take a day off to celebrate. Picking up one passenger after another, he slowly started to fade.

What is the point? Can I really be a taxi driver forever? Am I never going to make enough money to help and take care of the people I care about? Should I stop now while I am still ahead? I don't see an end in sight.

Getting his citizenship took away my father's ability to dream that he could become anything he wanted. He had desires to become a mechanic and maybe even open up his own business one day, but those dreams felt like an imaginary reality because becoming a citizen made him realize that the only place he stood in the American food chain was at the bottom. Every passenger that sat in his taxi made him realize that no matter how hard he tried or what he became, people will always see him as one thing: a broke, foreign taxi driver.

Unable to turn off his suffering, my father endured immensely. The mental health of immigrant parents is toxic, scary, and lonely. In the South Asian community, mental health doesn't exist. Imagine feeling unstable and depressed and thinking something is wrong with you instead of realizing that it's okay to feel that way. You don't have the internet to look up your symptoms. You can't talk to your wife about it because you don't want her to worry about the thoughts that keep you up at night. You can't talk to your family back home in India. You absolutely can't talk to your taxi friends; they won't think you are man enough to achieve the American dream.

The reality is that sadness can't hide. It comes out in different ways, no matter how hard you try to suppress it. The battles my father experienced were harsh and hard to face. After my brother was born, my father was alienated from his brother because they walked out on us. He couldn't turn to his in-laws; that relationship felt formal. Even if he helped them come to America, he couldn't ask for their help. In the South Asian community, you can't just turn to your wife's family for help without sacrificing a part of your masculinity. He promised to protect them, not ask for help from them. That's not how an Indian marriage works. It's because of that cultural friction he felt like he didn't have any other family in America. He couldn't just call them and ask for advice if he needed it. And when he would call India, he didn't want to disturb his mother's peace, so he wouldn't tell her what he felt. He didn't want his mother to worry about her sons in America. My father fought his battles alone, and his emotions became outward manifestations of sadness.

THE STAIN OF ALCOHOL

LIVING IN AN ALCOHOLIC FAMILY IS PUZZLING. AS A CHILD, you live on eggshells. Your father seems fine, happy, and even, sometimes downright silly when he has had a few too many drinks. When someone resorts to alcohol, it is almost always a reaction to something or someone causing them pain. But it can be difficult for the South Asian community to see that. The community is a results-driven society. We theorize and obsess over the result of any situation, regardless of whether it is good or bad. The community tends to focus on the result (alcoholism) and ignores the cause (poor mental health) because sometimes it's too complicated to try to understand.

In the South Asian immigrant community, mental health is considered a fabrication and an unacceptable excuse to not hold down the fort for your family. My parents grew up hiding their suffering. Their suffering was unacceptable, and if it made a visual appearance, it would be instantly dismissed and rationalized as the card that life dealt them. My mother is an outspoken person, so she internalized her mental health battles by suppressing her voice. My father is naturally quiet and reserved. To deal with his invisible battles, he turned to liquid courage: alcohol.

In the Punjabi community, drinking alcohol is associated with being masculine and powerful. Alcohol is seen as a birthright. You grow up around alcohol. All the Punjabi songs are about alcohol. Alcohol is medicine—a shot of brandy is the cure for the common childhood cold. Fathers idealize when they can have their first drink with their sons. The women know better than to ever drink alcohol. Every problem, every happiness, every event is celebrated with alcohol. Alcohol is your best friend. It's your first line of defense when things go wrong and your victory dance to celebrate the fruits of your labor.

My father grew up in a culture where alcohol was glorified as a necessity to live. It's almost as critical as breathing. He grew up with alcohol in India. He confided in alcohol during his voyage to America. He celebrated with alcohol when he got there. He held on to alcohol when he was lonely. He celebrated with alcohol when he got his first job. He poured his soul into alcohol, nervously waiting for my mom to come to America. He painted the town red during his youth with alcohol. He always turned to God and alcohol to help him, love him, and console him whenever he needed. That became his life. The foundation of my normalcy as a child was alcohol—something that was understood as dad's crutch to achieve success.

I didn't really notice a problem until my childhood started to get confusing. I was afraid of each day, and I didn't know what was going to happen next. At this time in our lives, our family faced a lot of unforeseen hardships. For one, my paternal grandmother died of diabetes, and now, my father had to live with the emptying truth that both of his parents were gone—a reality that takes a child a whole lifetime to come to terms with. My dad brushed off another tragedy, ignored his feelings, and started silencing his sorrows even more by hiding them.

He hid his pain by throwing himself into manual work. He started to work longer and harder, until every single waking hour became a curse. His internal struggles ran so deep that he didn't know how to process his emotions. The truth is, when we are unhappy, we travel back in our minds. My dad started to ruthlessly think about all the *what ifs*, what could have been, and what is now. Unhappy and unsure how to fix his suffering, he resorted to the only thing he knew could help him as a Punjabi man: he turned to alcohol to bury his emotions, the same way he buried both of his parents.

My first interactions with alcoholism scared me. I didn't know when my dad would be set off. I didn't know when a good conversation would turn sour. I walked on thin ice at home. I learned to be respectful, quiet, and kept to myself. I remember one night waking up to the sounds of pandemonium and panic. It was three o'clock in the morning. Our apartment door was open. Mom and Dad were nowhere to be found. My brother and I were so confused that we left the apartment and went downstairs into the apartment lobby. What we saw next still haunts me today.

There was a cop car. My dad's arm was bloody. There were several people from the apartment complex outside. I was confused and very scared of what was going on. My mom noticed my brother and me peeking through the frosted door. She came inside to tell us...

Go to sleep. Dad punched a car door. It's okay, we're going to figure it out. Nothing is going to happen. Go upstairs. Go back to sleep.

Confused and not sure what that even meant, my brother and I went back upstairs. We stayed upstairs for about five minutes before we turned restless and came back down. This time we were smarter; we hid in the hallway so that they couldn't see us. We peeped through the frosted glass door to see what was happening for short intervals and then quickly hid behind the corner, so we wouldn't be caught. We would take turns looking. I feared the shadow I saw behind me until I realized it was my own.

We stayed downstairs for an hour, trying to see what was happening. As soon as we saw the police car lights turn off, we ran upstairs and pretended we were sleeping. We had mastered the art of pretending to sleep. When my parents came upstairs, my dad went straight to sleep, and my mom came to check on us in the living room. She hugged us and sat there for the longest time. I think she sat there the whole night; I'm not sure. All I know is that I could sense her presence, and I was trying my hardest to pretend I was sleeping. Before I knew it, I had dozed off, and my mom was waking me up to get ready for school.

Me: *Mom, what happened?*

Mom: *Nothing. Dad got mad; he punched a car window, but it's fine. There was some problem with parking. He parked in someone's parking spot in the complex.*

Me: *Why? What happened?*

Mom: *Nothing. Get ready for school; we don't have time for this.*

Even after their parents hush them up, children wonder. They wonder what happened and why they feel funny. All I knew was that what Dad did didn't make any sense.

Why would he do something like that? Was he mad? Was it because of alcohol? Is he going to do that again? Every night? Why won't Mom tell me the truth? Did Mom make him mad? Did we do something wrong?

I don't remember what I learned in school that day because all I could think about was what happened and why.

I came back home that day, and everything seemed normal. I thought maybe there was something wrong with me, and I was being overly emotional. I told myself that everything was fine. Even though I was mentally telling myself it would be okay, my heart wouldn't believe me. My stomach felt weird. I just *knew* something was wrong. I was now battling myself as a child, trying to tell myself that everything was normal, even though deep down in my gut, I knew something was wrong.

For the next few couple of years, my brother and I battled this feeling. We couldn't really piece together what was going on. All we knew was that there were fights. A lot of them. Sometimes, my family fought with each other. Sometimes, they fought with our extended family. Sometimes, they even fought with their friends. We became aware of silence that was scary. Whenever we heard a loud noise, we automatically tried to sense if our parents were mad or if they were laughing. We stayed emotionally alert, so we could sense which outburst was coming next.

We had random conversations with my mom about what was happening. Sometimes, she would tell us the full story; sometimes, she would hide the details. Sometimes, other family members came in to help my parents. I remember my extended family came from out of town to talk my mother and father out of a divorce. I didn't know what "divorce" meant. I just knew my mom and dad weren't happy, and they wanted to live separately. In the end, they said they weren't going to have one. They told us that they wanted to stay together for us. They were here in America for us, and they would stay married to provide for us and our future.

We were not sure if that was good or bad news, but my brother and I felt like maybe we did something right. Since we were their children, they would stay together to keep us happy. Isn't that every child's dream come true when they learn their parents won't get divorced? We accepted that our family wasn't going to fall apart and tried to carry on. Not getting a divorce was one of the many difficult choices my parents made raising us, one day at a time.

As a child, I was oblivious that I was experiencing an adverse childhood experience. What is an adverse childhood experience? It's living through any type of abuse, neglect, or household dysfunction during your childhood. I didn't really know I was experiencing household dysfunction because that was my normal. I grew up feeling paranoid. Afraid of violence. On edge. Figuring out if I had to fight or flee. My brain grew up on this constant rush of adrenaline. I was always alert and ready to make a move. That may or may not be one of the reasons why I was driven to find a way out of that blue-collar life. My quest to find a way was the biggest blessing in disguise that my blue-collar family could have given me.

FOLLOWING A GUT FEELING

AFTER SEEING WHAT WAS HAPPENING TO MOST OF THE older kids in the area, my dad woke up one day and told my mom that we were going to move to Baltimore. His taxi driver friends would tell him stories of how their children had become "too American." They were starting to not care about their studies. They all had boyfriends and girlfriends. They went out to clubs and drank. They treated their parents disrespectfully and didn't care about their parents' sacrifice. My dad's friends were afraid that their kids were forgetting their roots and picking up the wrong American trait of individuality.

My dad made up his mind; he couldn't keep his family here anymore. His kids were not going to end up like these children too. He told his wife that within two weeks, they were going to move to Baltimore.

Mom: *Baltimore? Why?*

Dad: *Because I don't want my kids to grow up being like the kids here. I don't want my girl to turn out to be a ho, and I don't want my son to be a player. We must leave the community here; it isn't good. Kids learn from the company they keep. I've given America so much of myself already; I can't set my kids up for failure.*

My mother told us the next day that we were going to move because the schools and the community were better in Baltimore. There wasn't a big Indian immigrant community there, but that was okay. Their children wouldn't be around people who looked like them. They wouldn't just blindly follow the footsteps of children who looked like them. Moving away from an immigrant community meant that their children would be around American children, and that was the point—to only pick up the American traits of being successful at school. Being the only brown children in the community would mean they would feel isolated at school and look for belonging at home.

As a child, I remember being told that we were moving to a new city and being told to tell my school friends goodbye. I didn't understand what was happening because I didn't understand the totality of human relationships. I didn't realize that I would never see these children, this school, or this community again. I naively went into my school on the last day with a smile, ready to say my cheerful goodbye. Saying, "Goodbye" was easy for me because I didn't have any friends at school. They were my classmates, but they weren't my friends. Because I was an Indian girl first, I wasn't allowed to make friends; my parents made that very apparent when I was growing up. Saying, "Goodbye" to a couple of classmates was easy; I was going to get some new ones in Baltimore.

The move to Baltimore didn't really hit me until we were in the cars with all our stuff. We rented a small moving truck, and my dad told me it would take around three and a half hours to get to our new home. We had gone down to Baltimore as a family the weekend before to pick out an apartment. To me, it felt like an upgrade. We were going from a one-bedroom apartment to a two-bedroom apartment with a living room, a dining room, and a kitchen. We had so much space and were so excited. We had a huge parking lot with lots of parking space. There were trees everywhere. Even the tap water tasted better. Baltimore made my family feel like we were moving out of the city and into a decent suburban home for our family.

Even though everything about Baltimore seemed amazing, leaving New York was still monumental. As a child in the car that was about to leave the only home I had ever known, I realized for the first time in my life that the place that I called home for nine years was no longer home anymore. It was the first time in my life that I started to understand the totality of human experiences. Nothing is permanent. Every experience is changing. The present becomes history immediately. Life moves on, and that is exactly what we were doing. I closed my teary eyes and thought, *This is for the best. I know so.* I opened my eyes and painfully said, "Goodbye" to the melting pot that I called home.

As an adult, I put myself in my dad's shoes and deeply admire his courage. If I wanted to move to a different state, I would have a very risk-averse plan. I would start by applying to jobs, looking at the cost of living in that state, see if I can open a business, and look at the best places to live. I would research everything about my decision to the T to make sure I'm not making an irresponsible choice.

My dad? His entire move to Baltimore was based on a gut feeling, an emotional feeling that something in his current community didn't feel right. That's fearless. I call this the pack-and-go concept of immigrant parents. It's a decision that is based on an emotional reaction to the environment and the living condition around it. It's this feeling that something isn't right, so they act on it immediately. It could be argued that this exact feeling is the biggest reason they ended up in America in the first place. This sheer willpower to be fearless and to be results-driven is one of the many attributes that I admire about the immigrant experience. So many of us are scared. Scared to take the next step in life. Scared we will be judged. Scared we aren't making the best decision because our choices are endless. We are mostly scared to death about failing in a world full of success and prosperity. What if our parents were scared? They probably were. Change is scary, regardless of where you come from and who you are. But what matters most in any scary experience is realizing that you will be okay. Seeing my parents be fearlessly young and then re-learning just how fearless they were as adults is the aspect of the immigrant experience I hold closest to my heart.

Part V

A FAMILY
DIVIDED

DREAMS ON CREDIT

THE DRIVE TO BALTIMORE TOOK FOREVER. I FELL ASLEEP
and woke up ten different times, and we still were not there.
My family was cramped and had no room to move in the car.
We stopped for one bathroom break at a rest stop, but that was
about it. The whole time my parents were worried about the big
box TV we had in the back of their friend's car. They drove extra
slowly, trying to make sure that the TV made it. As soon as we
parked the car outside of the apartment and opened the trunk,
the TV fell out and broke. My father sighed and thought, *Great,
another thing I can't afford*. He turned to his family and told them
that he would find a smaller TV for them before he left for New
York on Sunday.

My father wasn't going to live with us in Baltimore. He was
going back to New York and planned on working there until
he could save up enough to move in with us. My father didn't
have the luxury of quitting his job and finding another one in
Baltimore, so his choices were limited. He decided that to pay
for our expenses in Baltimore, he would need to stay behind
in Queens and drive the taxi to support us. My father stayed in
New York for another year before he could financially afford to

be with his family in Baltimore. He felt okay leaving us in Baltimore because my mother's sister-in-law (Mamiji) had recently started to live with us in New York. Mamiji was already a US citizen and lived in California when she married my mother's brother; after marriage, she moved to live with the only in-laws she had in America, my mother. Now she had come with us to Baltimore, and my father felt confident that the four of us could figure it out together. Even though he believed in us, we were scared and had to come to terms with the reality of the type of life we lived now—where our father was absent.

When my father left Baltimore, his departure was hard for us—especially my brother. He had tears running down his face as he approached him before he left.

Brother: *Papa, why do you have to leave us here?*

Papa: *For your good study. I know it's hard, but it's for the best.*

Brother: *But, Papa, I don't want to be without you. Can you please stay?*

Papa: *I'll be back sooner than you know, but right now, you need to focus on your studies. Keep your mind sharp like the bald eagle.*

Brother: *Papa, if Baltimore is for our good study, does that mean I can be whatever I want to be?*

Papa: *Yes, beta, you can be whatever you want to be.*

Brother: *Even the president of the United States?*

Papa: *Anything. Just focus and do your best.*

Brother: *Okay, Papa. I'll miss you. Please come every weekend.*

Papa: *I'll try.*

Seeing Dad's car fade as we watched him drive away made one thing crystal clear—he was sacrificing his present so we could have a better future. Getting educated is the only way pat to prosperity in America.

Arriving in Baltimore was fun also. I remember unpacking. Running around the apartment like a dog in its new home. We had a living room in our one-bedroom apartment in Flushing, but the living room was my bedroom. We bought new stuff for our bedrooms and bathrooms. I remember feeling excited going to Carney Elementary with my mother when we went to give them all the papers they needed to enroll us in school. Our bus would stop right in front of our apartment complex. Baltimore felt new. My mother finally gained the confidence she needed to drive in Baltimore. She took us to the grocery store, to Walmart, to the mall—any place you can think of. We went with my mother everywhere she went because where else would we go? We didn't have the immigrant apartment community in New York anymore. My mother was struggling to establish roots in our new town, even if she didn't let us know. I remember eavesdropping on a conversation I overheard my parents having...

Yeah, we can try to limit the grocery bill, but everything is so expensive here. Yeah, I know. Have you thought about when you're coming again? Okay, that's fine. We're fine; don't worry. We'll manage.

I couldn't hear my father's side of the conversation, but I knew what he was saying. He was telling her to be brave and hold down the fort. He would be there as soon as he could. As a child, I never once thought about how he felt being alone in New York without his family. *Was he happy? Did he feel alone? Was he tired?* My father was out of sight and out of mind. Not just for me, but for everyone in my family. He started to become the hidden support system that our family knew was there but couldn't see anymore.

The American dream is complicated. The biggest problem with the American dream is that it cannot be achieved instantly. It takes time. It takes patience, and sometimes, all you want to see are small signs that you are on the right path. Not receiving validation and still working your ass off is a hard burden to carry. Because you're unable to see results instantly, many people in the immigrant community turn to anything that gives them a sense of fulfillment. For my parents, that fulfillment came from buying materialistic goods for their children that they knew they couldn't afford now but hoped they eventually could. Whether those goods be a toy, an item of clothing, or a book, they were rationalized as a need and bought on credit, a credit that fed the fire that was their hope. A hope that one day they will make more money to pay for whatever object they bought for their future, which, in this case, was their children.

Buying materialistic goods on credit to make us temporarily happy is an American trait that my parents learned as a product of living here: buying happiness for your children when you can't afford to sit with your own feelings of invisibility. My brother and I were aware that we didn't have that much money. We didn't understand how much we had, but we knew we didn't have enough. When we gave the cafeteria lady our student IDs for lunch at school, our lunches would ring up as free/reduced. I would look over my shoulder to make sure none of the other kids saw because I didn't want to be treated differently. When my Mamiji had her son, we learned that there were specific types of food you can buy with our special coupons, known as "food stamps." Time and time again, America was helping us, but we felt ashamed. Why couldn't we afford certain things? Were we doing something wrong being in America? As a family, we started feeling like we weren't enough to obtain the American dream because we didn't have enough.

BLUE-COLLAR CULTURE

IN BALTIMORE, MY MOTHER AND MAMIJI STRUGGLED WITH BEING isolated and not having a community here. In New York, they had other blue-collar Punjabi immigrant families who became their beacons of Punjab. Here in Baltimore County, they couldn't find anyone that even looked like them. Everyone was white or black. They couldn't find any Indian people. If they did find Indian people, they weren't the kind of Indian we were. The internet wasn't developed enough that they could just Yelp the nearest Punjabi hangout spot. They felt lost, alone, and for the first time ever in America, foreign. In New York, they saw people from all walks of life. Baltimore County felt different because they couldn't find anyone that looked even remotely like them.

One day my brother was out riding his bike around the apartment complex. He came home out of breath:

Brother: *Mom! Mamiji! I found a Punjabi auntie! I told her to wait outside so she can meet my Mom and Mamiji.*

Mom and Mamiji together: *What are you talking about? Why are you talking to strangers?*

Brother: *She's Punjabi. She has two little boys I can play with. You must meet her.*

They both got dressed briskly to go downstairs to meet this mysterious auntie. When they finally saw the auntie, they were pleasantly surprised. She was Punjabi. She lived in the same apartment complex community we lived in, and her apartment was a three-minute walk from ours. Not only did my family become instant friends with this Punjabi auntie, but she opened the door for my family to start feeling like maybe Baltimore could become our new home. She told us where the Punjabi Indian stores were and even told us where the gurdwara was. Having a community is critical to feeling like you belong, even if that community is just one family.

Even though we found a community, my mother and my aunt were having a hard time finding an employer who would understand their unique request—they wanted to work opposing schedules, so they could take care of us. They would spend all day applying to every job they could find. After trying for weeks, they found a job at Wendy's. Not only was Wendy's two miles from our home, but the management agreed that my mother would do the morning shift, and Mamiji would do the night shift. That way, we didn't need a babysitter, and someone could pick us up and drop us off at school if needed.

By the grace of God, my family figured out how to balance a work environment that knows no boundaries—a blue-collar job. Immigrants working blue-collar jobs give themselves fully and completely to their work. They believe in their ability to succeed as much as they believe that they will live to see another day. Immigrant families are always compromising their well-being, whether that be mental or physical, to provide structure to their family. One of the biggest compromises I saw was how my parents and Mamiji hardly slept. My dad would call at all hours of the day, and I always thought, *When does he sleep?* My mom and Mamiji would sleep only four to five hours, even though they had opposing schedules to take care of us. Sometimes, we would notice them snoozing in the car before they came to pick us up from school or an afterschool activity. We thought they were being silly or old. I didn't realize then that they were falling asleep in a hot car waiting for us because their bodies were exhausted from taking care of us.

Even though it was one of the hardest times of their lives, I remember this period of my life being an adventure. We were excited that our mom and Mamiji were working at Wendy's. They would bring home free food all the time. Growing up, having family work in a fast-food restaurant was amazing. We were able to try out all the new seasonal items for free. The fondest memory we had growing up was spending our summers at Wendy's. Sometimes, when the store was short-staffed, both Mom and Mamiji were scheduled to work the same shift. They couldn't tell their management no because they needed the money. The bigger problem: where would we go? They couldn't afford a babysitter.

My mom and Mamiji came up with a perfect solution. They asked their general manager if they could bring us to work. They promised we would stay in the lobby area the whole time, and we would be working on our homework, not disturbing the customers. They indicated that we were responsible children and would also take care of our baby cousin. The manager agreed, and we were on the best adventure ever—staying at one of our favorite fast-food restaurants all day long!

We proved we were respectful, and then coming to work with them became a regular occurrence. Staying at Wendy's during our summer break from school was exceptionally great because right across the street was White Marsh Mall. If we did our summer reading and homework, my mom and Mamiji would give us twenty dollars to spend at the mall. I remember walking over to the mall with our fun money and buying a book or a toy. It was the most exhilarating experience of my childhood. We felt like mini adults. Wendy's became our home. We felt safe. We felt American. The crew members even started feeling like family because they remembered our birthdays and would give us birthday cards.

Thinking about this experience as an adult, it dawns on me that I never felt embarrassed as a child that my family worked blue-collar jobs. To me, they seemed like your ordinary caretakers trying to make it in America. As a child, I decided that I belonged wherever my parents spent most of their time in America. My roots were the places they worked. Culture is a feeling that can live anywhere; it doesn't have to be tied to ethnicity. My culture became blue-collar work. I identified working hard as part of my identity. I wanted to be just like them. It wasn't until I started maturing into an adolescent child that my thinking started to change, possibly for the worst. I started to realize that my family members weren't those societal "Smart Indians," and I started to develop an identity crisis.

"SMART INDIAN"

Other kids: *You're Indian?*

Me: *Yes.*

Other kids: *So, you must be really smart.*

Me: *I don't know.*

Other kids: *What do your parents do?*

Me: *Why?*

Other kids: *They must be doctors, lawyers, or something successful.*

Me: *Huh?*

Other kids: *Don't be shy; tell us what your parents do for a living. Indian people are usually rich.*

Panicking, I thought, *Do they know my secret? Hurry up, think of a cover-up.*

Me: *I think my dad owns his own business.*

Other kids: *See, I knew it! Indian people are always smart. Your dad is an entrepreneur.*

Relieved, I took a deep breath.

It's not like these kids were going to come to my home and see where I lived or discover what my family did. Owning a cab is having a business…right? But saying that my father was a taxi driver made me feel like I wasn't normal and that something was wrong with my family because we weren't those Indians everyone in society was talking about. We weren't those "Smart Indians." We weren't those "Rich Indians." Nobody in my family was a doctor. We had one or two lawyers, but they were back home in Punjab, and they weren't rich. Nobody in my family owned a business, at least not yet. We weren't those Indian people that American society thought we were.

Even in the South Asian community, we couldn't openly admit that our family didn't come from educational or economical privilege. We knew better. We concealed our identity. It was extremely hard to hide my identity when I started going to Catholic school. Everyone there came from money and seemed well off. My family didn't come from a long line of professional careers. The privilege that my family had was different. We were from Punjab, and we had land. How do I tell the world that? Who moves to America to be a cab driver or be a fast-food cashier? How do you communicate to people that you want nothing more than to be that "Smart Indian"? That the purpose of my life in America is to be exactly just that: a smart, white-collar professional. Being from a blue-collar family constantly made us feel like we weren't enough to our Indian or American communities. My race defined what was expected of me, and those expectations were obvious with every single person who asked me, "Who are you and where did your family come from?" Everywhere I went, I constantly fought my stereotype. School was the first place I started fighting that "Smart Indian" stereotype because becoming a "Smart Indian" was exactly what I wanted to be.

APART

WE ALL HAVE DARKNESS IN OUR SOULS THAT WE TRY TO hide. Some people bury their truth by telling jokes instead of talking about what really hurts them. Some pretend everything is fine. Others are outright violent, and some internalize their pain and believe something is wrong with them.

Even though moving to Baltimore was the best decision for his family, it didn't always feel right to my father. Awareness and action of any decision are two distinct feelings. My father took immediate action when he saw that other immigrant children in the New York neighborhood were not taking education seriously. He moved his whole family to Baltimore and decided to stay behind in Queens alone. Alone in his misery to try to make more money. Alone, trying to figure out if any of this was worth it. Alone with his own thoughts and his own darkness, trying to be stronger for his wife and kids, hundreds of miles away. When he had his family with him, he enjoyed being with them and watching his kids grow. Now, his only source of happiness was away from him, and his emotions became mountains he couldn't move. There would be days when he didn't have the energy to continue and would be in a deep state of isolation and depression. It was on those days that he would decide to drive down to Baltimore and surprise his family. He would buy ten, if not more full-sized candy bars for his daughter and son, just to see them smile. Getting there and seeing his wife and children smile brought him joy, but that joy was temporary. When he left to go back to New York, his darkness was back. He was alone again and left to fight his own battles.

On his drives back to New York, all my father did was think—think about if this was the right decision. He would talk himself out of his fear of failure. He would remind himself that there is no one he could turn to who could provide strength. He had to carry on. Even if he didn't have the strength in himself, he had to build it. He had to try. After all, he was the one who brought his family here in the first place. At the end of these mental battles, my father always found the will to continue, regardless of how helpless he felt. Until one day, he decided he couldn't take it anymore. It was earlier than he had planned, but he couldn't take the isolation anymore. He sold his taxi license to be in Baltimore with his family. There was no amount of money that could make him stay now. He was well on his way to his own adventure—finding a new job in a new place.

KNOWLEDGE DESERVES RESPECT

MY FATHER'S FIRST JOB IN BALTIMORE WAS WORKING AT Papa John's in East Baltimore City. Papa John's was a dream come true for us. We loved pizza, and we joked that the pizza place knew that our dad was our father because my brother's name has "John" in it. He would always bring us home a pie of pizza on the days he worked. He would give us ten dollars of candy money from his tips. We thought dad loved his new job, but we were far from the truth. Working at Papa John's was killing my father's spirit. After twenty years of employment in America, working as a delivery man at Papa John's made him feel like it was his first day in this country again. He felt ashamed, embarrassed, and that his life was going nowhere. Working as a delivery man paid nowhere as well as being a taxi driver did, and as a taxi driver, he felt like he was his own boss. Being a taxi driver meant you could make your own schedule and go to work whenever you wanted; nobody could control how much you could work. Here at Papa John's, he had a schedule; he couldn't work longer hours even if he tried, and that irritated him. Feeling helpless and second guessing his decision for the *second* time, my dad turned to alcohol to soothe his insecurities.

My dad drank his heart out in Baltimore, and I mean *drank*. When I think about my childhood, there isn't a moment in my life where my dad wasn't drinking. My father would use his liquid courage to fact-check us to see what we were learning. He would ask us random questions he stumbled on in the newspaper or on TV. When we didn't know the answers to these questions, my dad would mock us.

Dad: *Why don't you know this? Why aren't they teaching you this in school? We are working hard to put you in school. Why don't you know this! Ask your teacher to teach you these things. You need to be successful.*

Us: *Okay, Papa.*

Depending on how much he had to drink, the questions he asked us would get harder. Sometimes he would ask us about the most random of facts that we had no way of knowing.

Dad: *What's the capital of Oklahoma?*

Me: *I don't know, Papa.*

Dad: *What do you mean you don't know?*

Me: *Sorry, Dad, I can look it up.*

Dad: *No, there is no point. You need to know the answer to every question, right away. How else are you going to get ahead?*

Me: *We didn't learn all the capitals in school yet; I think we will soon.*

Dad: *Are you talking back to me?*

Me: *No, Dad, I'm saying we didn't learn that yet.*

Dad: *You did it again.*

Me: *No, Dad, I'm saying I will learn about the capitals soon.*

Dad: *I said stop talking back to me.*

Frustrated because we wouldn't listen to his advice, my dad would hit us to make sure we understood that there was no talking back to elders. We learned to never question authority and to always comply.

Although his treatment of us may seem unfair, it came from a place of earnestness. What my father was trying to teach us is that knowledge is the key to our success. No fact is too little or big to know—he wanted us to be knowledgeable. My dad knew that knowledge is the only way up in America. He was disappointed that we didn't realize that. Sometimes, his friends or family would ask him questions about a topic he didn't know the answer to. He would reach out to us, the only literate dictionary he knew, to see if we knew the answer. If we didn't know, he had nobody else to turn to, to ask that question. Sure, it seems like a big burden to carry as a child learning about the world. But was it really? He wanted us to be the smartest Indians he knew because he never felt smart. Every job he worked, every place he visited, he was constantly reminded that he lacked intelligence. If you are in an environment where you are constantly told you aren't intelligent, you start believing it, even if it's incorrect. We were his aspiration of success. He couldn't become smart now; it was too late for him. But for us, he still had hope.

My father didn't have the time to get an education; he was

too busy providing for us. However, he hoped that one day his children could be the most well-known and smartest kids in his community. I was okay with providing that to him because I wanted nothing more than to be that too. He wanted us to study; that seemed a lot easier to do then providing for a family. I learned quickly to make knowledge a part of my identity because that was something my dad dreamed of. If I became knowledgeable, it would not only benefit me but my parents too. You can achieve anything if you work hard; my dad was living proof of that. Maybe through me, we could both achieve this dream of knowledge together.

HIDING A SECRET

AFTER I GRADUATED FROM ELEMENTARY SCHOOL, MY mother decided that I was going to a private Catholic school. There were several factors that went into her decision of enrolling me in that type of school, but the biggest reason was: I was a girl, and because of that, I needed to go to a strict school. She didn't want me to go to an all-girl's school because she wanted me to know how to socialize with boys, but she wanted to make sure that if I was learning how to socialize with boys, I had supervision. What better school than a religious school that believes in saving yourself for marriage, right? Now that I was becoming an adolescent, my mother wanted to make sure she protected me as much as she could from growing up. My enrollment into a Catholic school was the first time I realized I was going to be raised differently than my brother because I was a girl.

Going to middle school is hard enough. Imagine going to an all-white middle school full of Catholic children, and you are the only brown person with a different religion. Literally. In sixth grade, I was constantly asked:

Where are you from? You look different. You're also a different religion because you're not wearing a cross. What are you? Hindu? Why are you at a Catholic school if you are Hindu? You're probably really smart because you're Indian. I'll sit next to you. Also, you're like, hairy; you should tell your parents you need to shave. American kids shave. You need to shave if you ever want a boyfriend.

Oh, my good God. Someone help me! Anyone.

Middle school felt different because I looked different. I didn't fit in. I stood out. I didn't know how to explain to the children that I was Sikh. I also couldn't figure out how to tell them that, in my religion, we don't shave our hair. Baltimore felt different because it wasn't religion-free like Flushing. Kids also thought I was a "Smart Indian." Nothing they thought about me was correct. Instead of correcting them, I let the kids think whatever they wanted about me, and I started to live up to the stereotype they thought I was. When you don't see yourself being represented in your surroundings and peer group, you realize you are different, and there is no one like you. Feeling alone is the single most heartbreaking thing a human can feel, regardless of how young or old you are.

My Catholic school education taught me that silence lets you become invisible. Once again, invisibility became an immigrant's shield and shelter; I wanted nothing more than to be invisible. To fly under the radar. I didn't want people to notice how I was different. I didn't want them to see I was hiding a secret. My secret being that I was not that "Smart Indian."

I did well in middle school, but I was still struggling with English. I didn't understand all the different rules of what makes up a sentence—why it's important to write a certain way and, most importantly, what it meant to write well. I didn't know how to pronounce my words still so I would only use the words I knew, which led to my solid straight *C*+ average in English. My parents were furious and didn't understand why I was doing so poorly. They were paying for a top-notch education. I should know this stuff because they were paying a monthly tuition.

The problem was I was scared to ask for help because I knew

it would cost more money, and we barely had enough to begin with. My principal would send me home with a note that said if my mom couldn't send the tuition money with me tomorrow, I couldn't sit in on my classes anymore. My mom did the only thing she knew how to do; she pawned her gold jewelry. Moreover, my school lunches (bologna and ketchup sandwiches) always looked different from the other kids' lunches, and I would beg my parents to get me Lunchables because it was American; I got them sometimes, and I felt guilty because I knew they were expensive. My point is I felt guilty, and confidence was something I had to learn on my own. I never felt confident at school. Nobody in my family knew what they were doing, and every decision we made as a family was based on necessity and limited knowledge. Nobody could teach me confidence because they weren't confident themselves. My father would repeatedly remind us that...

Education is the most important thing. You only have right now to get educated, and if you don't put your whole heart into studying, you will never become successful. We sacrificed our whole lives for you to get the best education you possibly could. Please don't let our sacrifices be in vain. Try your hardest.

How could you feel confident when you are hiding a secret? I needed help in school so I could become that "Smart Indian," but there was nobody I could turn to.

IMMIGRANT WORK ETHIC

AFTER A WHILE, PAPA JOHN'S WASN'T WORKING FOR MY
dad, so he made up his mind that he needed to make a change.
He started looking at different liquor stores, convenience stores,
restaurants--honestly, any small business or restaurant that he
could potentially lease or buy. My dad had enough money for
half of the cost of a business, so he started to see if there was
anyone who would like to go into partnership with him. He
wasn't going to start with family because family had been tough
on him, especially after New York.

My dad decided to reach out to his restaurant friend in Baltimore to see if there was anyone he knew who would be willing
to go into business with him. After a few weeks, he found an
Indian man who was willing to be his partner. This man had
a lot of experience working in a restaurant, was a hard worker,
and had enough money to go in half with my father. Pretty soon,
they both started looking around for small mom-and-pop shops
to lease. Finally, they settled on a small restaurant called Star
Express, located a few blocks away from the Broadway Market in
Baltimore City. The restaurant had potential because it was in
an up-and-coming neighborhood, even though it didn't seem

like that now. After a few weeks of negotiation, my dad finally had his own business—a small, quick American food restaurant in Baltimore City. Baltimore was starting to look up.

Star Express was a blast. My dad seemed happy again. Everyone was helping, including us. We would clean the dining area of the restaurant. We would also go on all types of errands with my dad after school or during the summer break. Our favorite errand was going to Jetro, also known as Restaurant Depot, a place for restaurants to buy food items in bulk. My brother and I would go down every aisle looking at the massive sizes for every food item you can imagine: ketchup, soda, bags of chips—anything you can think of, they had it in bulk.

Our favorite aisle was the snowball aisle. During summer vacations, my dad would let us have our own snowball stand outside of the restaurant. We would pick all the flavors we wanted from Jetro, along with marshmallows and ice, to make the snowballs. We took our small business very seriously and would take turns selling snowballs to people walking down the streets of Broadway in Fells Point. Maybe we ate more than half of the snowball supplies we had, but for whatever it was worth, we felt responsible and were having fun.

My dad would warn us to be careful and not to leave our small Styrofoam cup of money on the table outside if we came in to eat something on our lunch break. Of course, we didn't listen to him, and we would forget constantly. One day, while my brother and I were on our lunch break, some man ran up and stole our cup of money. We tried running after him, but he ran so quickly that we lost track of what direction he went in. We came back to tell our dad that we didn't catch him.

My dad laughed and said...

Told you to be careful. Listen next time.

We were so mad! Why would someone come and steal our snowball stand money? Granted we didn't make that much, and the money was mostly so we could go down the street to buy something at Rite Aid, but still, we worked hard for it. Sitting out in the sun on a hot Baltimore day, just to make enough money to get a few snacks and some chocolate. Reminiscing on this memory as an adult, I am amused by our stupidity to leave the money outside in the middle of Baltimore City. What were we thinking? We got over it soon and learned to be better with money, even if it was a few dollars.

* * *

Even though things were looking up for my dad, that didn't mean things were completely okay in other parts of our lives. My mother was now an assistant manager at McDonald's. The extra money seemed like a blessing because Star Express wasn't breaking even yet. My mom really liked her new job and her new position. She took her new responsibility seriously, and everyone saw it. I think it was the first time in her life that I saw her being passionate about where she worked. Making money—no matter how much—can make a South Asian woman feel like she has purpose in life. Even if that purpose is a moving target to make more money for your family. She would work every and any shift McDonald's wanted her to work because she was the breadwinner of our family now. There's nothing she wouldn't do for her job.

One day, my mom was opening the store. While she was checking on things in the back office, a man came in to rob the store at gunpoint. Yes, a real, live, loaded gun. A gun that the robber could use to kill her. When my mother came to the front of the store, he put the gun to my mom's head and told her to open the cash register. She complied and opened it. He then directed her to take him to the safe at the back of the store. She listened and took him. As soon as she opened the safe for him, he quickly started putting the money in his bag. When she was opening the safe, she quickly pressed the button underneath the table that would alert the police to come to the store. The man was so busy putting the cash away that he forgot he left the gun on the counter. My mom noticed the placement of the gun immediately. She took a deep breath and did what she knew best. She started to fight. She started to kick the living crap out of him. Literally. She violently kicked and kicked and kicked everywhere she could on his body until he couldn't take it anymore and ran out of the store. He ran out of the store without his gun and the money he hoped to steal. He was so shocked by what had transpired, he ran out with nothing because that is how scary my mom was.

When the police arrived, they were stunned when my mom told them what happened and how he left. The police reminded her that he could have literally shot her. My mom responded by saying...

He didn't now, did he? I'm still alive. I'm not letting anyone take advantage of me and how hard I work. I am the manager of this store, and I will protect it no matter what.

The police officers told her to be careful next time; if someone has a weapon; she should not retaliate. My mother indicated she understood, but deep down, she was telling them what they wanted to hear. That wasn't the only time my mom was robbed at gunpoint. She was robbed a dozen times throughout her career as a manager at McDonald's. Every single time, she fought. Why? Because in America you fight for what is right. She fought for the job that was giving her everything. She fought because she wanted to give back to the job that was giving her everything. As a first-generation American, you fight for every job, every corporation that gave you a chance. That employer becomes your family. Work becomes your family. And that is the contribution my mom made at that McDonald's. She treated that job as if it was her own business. That is the immigrant work ethic the media doesn't talk about. That is the immigrant work ethic that builds the foundation of our economy in America. Year after year. Century after century.

BROWN, HAIRY, AND DIFFERENT

MIDDLE SCHOOL DIDN'T START OFF AWFUL. I HAD SOME friends. I was even invited to sleepover parties with a few girls in my class. I had people who would remember my birthday and ask me how my day was going. And then 9/11 happened. The events of September 11 changed everything, everywhere for brown people. When 9/11 happened, I was at an all-white Catholic school, and it was far from pretty. I was the only brown kid that those kids knew, and I was reminded every day that I was a terrorist. It didn't matter if I held the door open for my classmates or helped the teacher after school. Whenever the other students were around me, they constantly reminded me that they saw me as one thing and one thing only—someone they were afraid of because of the color of my skin.

My life in middle school was "Before 9/11" and "After 9/11." Overnight, people went from liking me to instantly hating me. I didn't understand their unwarranted hatred for me. It's not like I knew any of the attackers that did this to our country. I felt constant hatred, and it made me miserable.

I felt ashamed when I looked at the color of my skin. I feared that the kids around me would hurt me because they couldn't understand me. Yes, some men in my family wore a turban, but that didn't make them terrorists. It didn't matter that we were Sikh and not Muslim. The point is that regardless of what religion you practice, or what race you are, that doesn't make you the terrorists that took the lives of thousands of innocent people. An irrational group of brown people don't represent an entire religion or a subcontinent of South Asians. *Just because I look foreign, please don't be afraid of me. I'm afraid of you being so afraid of me.* America was my home; it was sad that people couldn't see that during this time in American history. It didn't matter if you were an American citizen. If you looked like someone that society was afraid of, you were automatically on the outside.

That was my whole experience in middle school. Nobody wanted to be my friend anymore because I looked different. Even if I tried to be like the other American kids, I slowly started to realize that no matter what, I would always be different.

I became shy and realized that I was my only friend. I asked myself...

Where did these kids grow up that they felt the constant need to be an asshole to people who looked different than them? They lived in the same country I did. Why did I think differently? What was so different about their upbringing that fostered hatred? Was it because they were rich, and I was poor? Why was I being treated differently?

In my head, I rationalized that one of the reasons I was being treated differently was because everyone figured out that I wasn't that "Smart Indian." My worst nightmare was when my father would pick me up from school. Not because it was him picking me up from school but because of the car he drove. He still drove the yellow cab from New York without the taxi license plates. To an outsider, it essentially looked like a cab. Every time my parents would pick me up from school, I would pretend that

I wanted to sleep in the backseat of the car. I would lie down, hoping that nobody would see me hiding. If they couldn't see me in the backseat, they wouldn't know it was me in the yellow cab. I would hold my breath, trying to be quiet, so the other kids couldn't hear me in the car either. I wanted so much to be unnoticeable that I literally pretended I *wasn't* in the backseat of my parents' car when they picked me up from school. Being young, I didn't have the foresight to realize that people could see my very brown parent in the driver's seat taking me home.

Because of the color of my skin, I was very visible, and I wanted nothing more than to hide. Around the time I hit puberty, hair started growing everywhere. Everyone in my school noticed my thick hair on my legs because I wore a uniform that required me to wear a skirt. If you're a South Asian woman, you know what I'm talking about. We are born with so much hair, it's unbelievable. Being a hairy middle school girl was just another way I didn't fit in. I tried to ignore how often I was bullied about my hair and would hide it for as long as I could from my parents. My parents were literally and figuratively working themselves to death—they had more important things to worry about than how I was feeling about being bullied.

I tried to be strong until one day, a boy told me to go to the boys' bathroom because of how hairy I was. I broke down. Kids are brutal, especially middle school kids. I felt ashamed and embarrassed that I couldn't control the amount of hair that was growing out of me. Feeling ostracized, I came home crying and asked my mom if I could shave my legs. She resisted. I begged and told her what happened. The answer was still no, for now. She said that maybe I could shave when I was a bit older, like in eighth grade. I had a full year to go. Even though it seemed far away, I was happy that the answer wasn't no. I started to count down. Since I went to a private school, I had to wear a skirt every day. I was thinking of workarounds to hide my legs. My legs were exposed during the hot weather. During the winter months, I could wear tights, so I technically had one more season of torture before eighth grade. Determined not to give up, I ignored everyone's comments and pretended that I didn't understand English. I would smile when kids said horrible things to me about my hair, and it confused them. I did have one thing going for me: I was foreign, and I could pretend that I didn't understand what they were saying to me, even if I did. I learned how to fake it until I made it. In this case, until eighth grade.

O SAY CAN YOU SEE?

NOT EVERYTHING WAS TERRIBLE IN MIDDLE SCHOOL. MY favorite memory was winning a Baltimore County essay on Americanism. I, the foreign kid in my all-white school, won second place for writing an essay about how brave Francis Scott Key was for writing "The Star-Spangled Banner" during the bombing of Fort McHenry in 1814.

I remember when we were told in English class that, for extra credit, we could write an essay about "The Star-Spangled Banner," and the teacher would submit it to Baltimore County for a contest. We would get five extra points in English and a chance at being selected to win. Given my straight-C+ average, I needed all the extra credit I could get, so I decided to write the essay. I remember going to the library and researching "The Star-Spangled Banner." The actual poem was beautiful, but I was especially drawn to just how brave Francis Scott Key was for experiencing the bombing. So, I decided that I would write about how brave he was to witness such a horrific time and still be able to create a poem beautiful enough to touch the souls of every single American today. I wrote that I aspired to be brave like him, especially in a time post 9/11. Not thinking twice or ever thinking that I could win the contest, I submitted my essay to my teacher, feeling grateful that I would get the five extra credit points.

Months later, my English teacher pulled me aside and told me that I won second place for my essay. I didn't believe her, and I told her that she had probably mistaken me with another student. She stressed, "No, they loved your essay!" They were even writing a letter to me, thanking me for being brave and inviting me to come to an award ceremony to share how I felt writing the essay. She also mentioned it came with a cash prize.

I held on to that smile I had after hearing the news all day. As soon as my mom picked me up from school, I told her I won a contest, and she showed she was incredibly proud of me by hugging me to pieces. She promised that we could go to Walmart to get some nice clothes. At Walmart, I picked out a nice dress, and my mom insisted that I wear a denim jacket to show off just how American I was. Nodding, I agreed and was excited to be able to go to the formal event to receive my prize.

Even though I'm pretty sure the structure of my sentences didn't make any sense, and I probably had typos, I still somehow won. I started to wonder how and why. I truly believed that there was a mistake until I saw the certificate that congratulated me with *my* name. Realizing that you've undersold yourself everywhere you have gone is an experience every poor and "not smart" person has felt. There are moments in life when you are reminded that effort is more important than ability. The little research I did on Francis Scott Key gave me all the direction I needed to make me feel like I could write a decent-enough essay to get five extra credit points for English. However, I undersold myself by not believing that I could write a winning essay, even though I literally just did. It's hard to be confident, especially when the world around you is throwing around signs indicating that they think you are a foreigner and then stereotyping you to be the Indian you aspire to be—that "Smart Indian." Throughout my life, I was reminded time and time again, that the little knowledge I had gave me all the direction I needed to make me feel like maybe I was on the right path to success. It guided me like an angel through my path of uncertainty. For that, I'll always be grateful.

SOUL ON FIRE

NOVEMBER 11, 2002—EARLY MORNING AROUND 6:00 A.M.—
my father's partner called and told him that the restaurant was
on fire. In complete shock, my father asked him to repeat what
he said. His partner repeated that there was a fire in the Rite Aid
next to the store. The Rite Aid, liquor store, and Star Express
had all burned down. The firefighters couldn't save the buildings.
Our whole world stood still. I woke up to my mom's cries. She
was praying. My aunt was sitting in a corner with her hand on
her forehead. My father was breathing heavily. My brother and
I had this sick feeling in our stomachs. You know that feeling
when you are about to go down on the roller coaster? Fear?
Yeah, we had that. We were afraid of what was going to happen
next. How were we going to handle this new stress as a family?
We quietly listened to our father explaining the story to us. We
had to accept what had happened, even if it seemed unfair.

In a moment, you can lose everything. My father had put
half of the money he made from selling the taxi towards that
restaurant, and now he couldn't help but think, *Was it even worth
it? What am I going to do for a living now? What about all the money we lost?
What about the cook and one employee that I hired? Why is God testing me again?
What did I do to deserve this? Why must I see failure, again and again?*

All the unanswered questions in his heart turned to anger.

He became angry that he was another vessel of disappointment when it came to the American dream. He was working as hard as he possibly could, and still, he was failing. Why was the American dream so hard to capture? Why did it seem so out of reach? Anger is the only emotion that working-class families can relate to. We use this emotion as a veil to hide our insecurities. When that veil lifts or betrays us with misfortune, we are destroyed and become angrier at the world around us. Sometimes it's hard to control your anger when you feel like you have been wronged for no reason. Anger destroys people in different ways. It hides the same way darkness hides in your soul. As a working-class family that just experienced misfortune, we didn't know where to go from here. The only thing we knew for sure was that it could only go up from here. We had to believe that—it was the only thing we had left.

A few months passed, and my father decided that the best thing he could do was go back to what he knew how to do best— drive. He started driving taxis for Baltimore City. It didn't pay as well as the taxi in New York did, but it was money, and he desperately needed it. After several months of driving the taxi, my dad still felt uneasy. He constantly thought about how he needed more money, but nothing was working out for him. He started to think deeply about what he was good at. He was good at driving. What type of driving could he do to make more money? There's only one answer to this question in the Punjabi blue-collar working community—drive a truck. My dad thought about driving a truck for a few months. He thought about it long and hard. He knew it involved a rigorous driving test and a written exam. He was nervous about the written exam, but he knew he could pass the driving test no matter what. A person gets better at driving with experience; all he had was experience. There was a huge drawback of driving a truck, though. He would live on the road, several days at a time, before he could come home and see his family. He would be spending days—even weeks—away from us, living on the road, traveling to different parts of America, to make more money for us.

Even though he was incredibly nervous about being alone again, my father thought he owed it to us to try. He studied for the driving test for months and passed his exam on the first try. For the first time in a long time, my dad felt confident. He felt maybe he could achieve success. Maybe everything he'd been through was a lesson to get him here. Maybe he was intelligent. Maybe he knew what he was doing for his family. Maybe all of this was for a reason, and maybe everything was going to be okay. There was only one way to find out—he had to try and be the best driver he could be.

Part VI

—

BECOMING

~~AN~~ ~~INDIAN~~

~~AMERICAN~~

GIRL

CHOSEN IDENTITY

PAYING FOR PRIVATE TUITION FOR THREE YEARS ALMOST put my parents in debt, so the obvious choice after middle school was getting into a good public school. My mother didn't want me to go to just any public school; she wanted me to go to the best magnet school in Baltimore County: Eastern Technical High School.

Eastern Tech was a great school, but I feared I wouldn't place into it. Eastern Tech had four major admission requirements, and one of those requirements was taking a math and English assessment. If I didn't place in Eastern Tech, I had no idea where I was going to go—maybe home school. I studied day and night for that math and English assessment because I didn't want home school to become my reality. After months of preparation, I finally took the exam and nervously waited for the news. The pressure of making sure I placed in Eastern Tech was unbearable; I constantly felt like I should be doing something else to prove to the admissions office that I should be given a chance, even though all I had to do was wait. Weeks went by. I didn't hear anything. It was almost time for summer break, and I had no idea if I was going to Eastern or not. When people asked me where I was going for high school, I would say, "Hopefully Eastern," and they would look at me with concern.

Kids: *You're going to a public school?*

Me: *Yes, well, it's a magnet public school.*

Kids: *It's a public school, though. Your parents don't have money to send you to Mercy or Institute of Notre Dame?*

Me: *No.*

By the time I graduated middle school, I had received no news. I accepted the fact that I was going to go to my local home school in my county. The first few weeks of summer break, I was miserable and nervous, but I tried not to think about it because I still had the whole summer to enjoy myself. Then one day, out of the blue, I got a letter from Eastern Tech that said that I had waitlisted! My number on the waitlist was in the teens, so the admissions office indicated that I could come in for an interview and schedule my orientation. Unbelievable. Somehow, I was smart enough to get into a magnet school. I'm not sure if it was my studying or that I went to a private school that helped me with my magnet school exam. Whatever the reason, I was grateful that I had a chance to become something, anything.

I didn't interact with other students during my high school orientation. I was a nerdy Indian girl with full-on facial hair who had perfectly symmetrical eyebrows. I decided that no matter what, I would not be that shy Indian girl I was in middle school. The first day of high school came, and I took a deep breath. I was determined to be outgoing. I went over to a group of girls and introduced myself—I told them who I was, what major I had chosen, and what I liked to do for fun. I was determined to make friends and let people see me for who I was on the inside: a girl full of hope and aspiration.

I started my high school transcript on a high—I was an A

student, and I was doing well enough in school that I started believing that I could be whatever I wanted. I felt confident enough to make friends and be myself. The smarter I felt, the more my confidence grew. As my confidence grew, so did my father's. He was becoming more confident driving the truck. My family started doing well enough financially to buy a house. It was the first time in our lives that we felt like we had enough. Driving a truck paid well, and the extra money allowed my family security to put a down payment on a house. My parents were now American homeowners. We had a roof over our heads that was ours. A place we could make our own. A sanctuary.

Even though, financially, things seemed okay, I was having a hard time adjusting between my personalities at home and school. The more I grew into understanding my own personality, the more I felt the need to censor myself. I didn't know how to control these emotions I was feeling as a teenager. My American and Indian identities were clashing hard against each other. America is about the individual. Indian culture is about the family. So, naturally, as I was trying to understand myself and define my own independence, my worlds collided. My parents always reminded me to follow in the footsteps of middle-class white Americans in school, so I could become successful. They were risk-averse Indian parents, and the media had scared the hell out of them with the rap videos and violence that they saw associated with other ethnicities and communities. Given that my race was defined by what I was expected to achieve, I never felt like I could be authentically myself around anyone. Imagine the pressure of trying to figure out what your dreams are and being constantly reminded that you need to accomplish the dreams your parents couldn't. It's the burden of feeling like your success and identity aren't yours alone but a representation of your parents' struggle and the identity that they gave up by being here in America for you. My identity became a realization of constantly fighting my thoughts and the culture around me and trying to figure out who I really was. Since I was told I could not assimilate into America's mainstream culture without jeopardizing my whole career, I looked for anything that could help me express my hyphenated identities and make sense of them.

What I found that made me feel like my struggle could be seen was rap music. Eminem, Nas, Tupac, Jay- Z, and 50 Cent spoke to me in their lyrics and in the way they described the challenges of being marginalized, living with nothing, and trying to make money for their families. Listening to rap music was the first time I felt like I was being heard about how I felt inside.

When I started liking rap music, my dad became terrified of what I was becoming in high school. In my bedroom, I had a giant poster of 50 Cent behind my door. Every time he saw it, he would express his disapproval as he walked out of my room. He constantly reminded me that I was not to like men or anyone like 50 Cent. When I got on the school bus, I would blast his music on my CD player because I felt like I could be myself since my parents weren't around to watch me. I was slowly starting to become successful (by doing well in school) while engaging in small acts of rebellion against my parents (by listening to rap music). I was starting to master the art of being a chameleon. I would filter my identity based on the group of people I was around. At school, I would show the American traits I identified with. At home, I only showed the traits my parents wanted to see. For the first time in my life, I started settling down and getting comfortable with my hyphenated identity.

"OF AGE"

HIGH SCHOOL WAS THE FIRST TIME I FELT COMFORTABLE telling people that my parents immigrated over to America. I would teach people how to pronounce my name and the meaning behind it. Even though half the people tried to give me an English nickname, I always corrected them and told them that my name was Sabreet because my parents worked too hard to make sure I had the correct name at birth. There were a dozen other South Asian kids at my school, so I felt like I found a place where I could be seen. I started voicing my opinions more at school. I started to notice that I would speak a lot more everywhere I went and that I was kind of funny. People would laugh at my jokes and wanted to be my friend. High school is where I started developing my authentic personality because, for the first time in my life, people started to see me for who I was. When I started high school, I made it known to my parents that I would be shaving, wearing normal clothes, and waxing my facial hair so that people could see beyond my appearance. I didn't want to be that hairy Indian girl anymore. I wanted to be a girl in high school. What I didn't account for was exactly that—being a *girl* in high school who looked attractive *and* had Indian parents.

The first time someone told me that I was sexy, I was puzzled because I thought they were either trying to make fun of me or talking about someone else. The first time someone told me, "You look pretty cute for an Indian girl...actually, you're sexy for an Indian girl," I had a million thoughts running through my mind. *I'm cute? Sexy?! He knows about other Indian girls too. Why does he think I'm prettier? Why did I giggle?* It was the first time in my life that I got butterflies. I felt like I was both insulted and, at the same time, given a compliment.

Even though there were guys who told me I was attractive and that they wanted to go out with me, I didn't feel like I could reciprocate any feelings. I wasn't supposed to like or talk to any boys. My mother told me that they were a distraction. The first time a boy told me that I was cute, I started thinking back to the first time I got my period and what my mother said. I didn't receive sex education. In the South Asian community, you don't talk about reproductive health or anything related to sexuality. I also didn't go to a public middle school, where sex education was mandatory for kids going through puberty—I went to a religious private school, where sex wasn't talked about; only abstinence was. The first time I had my cycle, I hid it from my mom for two days. I genuinely believed I was dying of stomach cancer. I didn't know why I was bleeding; all I knew was that I was using all the toilet paper in our house. I would stuff my underwear with as much as I could. I would wipe down there forever, hoping it would go away. But it didn't, and I reached a point where I felt like I had to tell my mom the truth.

I waited until she was out of the shower. Her hair was wrapped in a towel. I was sitting at the dining table, waiting to tell her my self-diagnosis. I didn't know what to say, so I yelled...

Me: *Mom, I'm dying! My private part is bleeding. I don't know what happened.*

Mom: *What?*

Me: *I'm bleeding down there, and I don't know why.*

My mom looked confused and then instantly scared.

Mom: *Sabi, you finally became a woman. Listen to me very, very carefully. You cannot talk, touch, or speak to boys.*

Me: *What?*

Mom: *Sabi, you just got your period; that means you can have a baby.*

Me: *How can I have a baby? I thought only grown-ups could have kids after they were married.*

Mom: *Sabi, I am telling you what to do, so you don't have one.*

Me: *What?*

Mom: *You can't talk to, touch, or even kiss a boy.*

Me: *Why would I do that anyway?*

Mom: *Because if you did, you would become pregnant and have a kid. You don't want that, right?*

Me: *No. But does that mean I can't talk to my brother anymore?*

Mom: *No, your brother is fine. Everyone else is not. Don't talk to them.*

Me: *Okay...*

I left that conversation feeling dumbfounded that I became a woman overnight without even realizing that I was going through this magical transition. One thing was clear, though: I couldn't talk to boys or have them touch me because I didn't want to become pregnant. I remember that when people joked about sex, I was confused, and I asked someone at school what sex was. She told me to look it up on the internet. She called me naïve and told me to stay that way for as long as possible. After I learned what it was, I wanted to make sure I never liked or dated a boy because I didn't know how people felt the need to do what I saw online. All I knew was that people get attracted to one another, and things happen.

When a non-Indian boy in high school told me I was cute, I said, "Okay." When a boy asked for my number, I didn't give it to him, or I would pretend I didn't hear him ask. In my small group of friends, there was a boy who liked me and had asked for my number. I thought if I ignored him, I would get away with it. Unfortunately, we had a mutual friend in common who happened to be a girl. I could talk to a girl, so obviously, I gave her my number. The only number I had was my house number because I didn't have a cell phone. So, when the boy asked for my number from our mutual friend, she gave the house number to him, not thinking twice. What happened next was straight out of an Indian soap opera. He called my house phone. My mother picked up. He asked for me. My mom cussed him out and hung up. Then, my mother stormed over to me and asked why a boy had called asking for me. Imagine my disbelief and shock.

Me: *What boy?*

Mom: *You tell me, Sabreet. A boy called this house asking for you. How do you not know?*

Wonderful. I now knew that my mother knew people found me attractive in school. I explained to her that I only gave my number to a few girls, and I will tell them that it's against my culture to talk to boys. She then reminded me that some girls are bad too; they are obsessed with boys, and they become teenage mothers, so I should watch out for girls like that as well. I nodded my head to comply, so I wouldn't get into any more trouble.

I went to school the next day, and the boy asked me what was up with my mom. I said I have strict parents. He understood and said he didn't have time to deal with that mess. I told him I wasn't interested anyway (because, seriously, I wasn't—I didn't want to be a teenage mom). I told my girlfriend that she couldn't give out my number; it was against my culture. She thought I was weird but understood.

Friend: *Parents are uptight in high school anyway. If you ever wanted to talk to a boy, let me know, and I can three-way you into a conversation with him if you wanted.*

Me: *Why would I do that? I'll get caught.*

Friend: *You can learn how to lie. It's not that hard.*

Me: *I'm not lying to them. That's ridiculous.*

Friend: *You worry too much. If you like a boy and you want to talk to him, lie and pretend you're talking to a girl. Fake it till you make it, girl.*

Not only did that girl corrupt me, but she also helped me see that there is a whole world of children out there who don't think about their very South Asian parents before deciding to like someone. Who knew?

I thought about lying for the rest of the school year. I could lie to my parents and tell them I was talking to a girl if I liked a boy. How insane is that? But my first interaction with a non-Indian boy taught me that they didn't want to deal with my drama.

Having strict parents was drama. Who would even want to like me if they knew I had strict parents? Not the boys at my high school. What about Indian boys? There weren't any Indian boys in high school that I thought would be interested in me, and I didn't know if they wanted to even deal with me. One thing was for sure: I liked being liked. Being liked by the opposite sex made me feel like I was loveable. It was the first time I ever felt love because of my gender. I wanted to feel that way again, but I didn't want to be a teenage mom. So, I decided the next best thing I could do was to look for a relationship online. It took away the physical aspect that would lead to children but would still give me that connection I was desperately looking for. I decided that if I was going to do something risky for the first time, I would do it over summer break. On the last day of school, I came home, went to bed, and said a short prayer...

God, I want to be loved. I want to find love. Can you please find someone for me? Someone tall, dark, and handsome like in the fairy tale movies. Please?

I closed my eyes extra tight and went to sleep.

That next morning, I decided that it was time to create a Myspace account. I created my AIM login and named it Kamli Kuri (Crazy Girl), looking for love in a space full of endless possibilities.

THE WILD, WILD WEB

CREATING MY MYSPACE ACCOUNT WAS SCARY AND LIBERating at the same. It was the first time I felt like I could fully be myself. My parents weren't on the internet to monitor me. I didn't have to connect with people at my school. I created my profile to be *me*. I could search and find people like me.

I took a selfie using my bathroom mirror, with the intention of looking friendly and cute. I uploaded it and started to work on my profile. I listed out all the rap songs I liked and my favorite movies and quotes that I thought represented me. Then I started customizing my Myspace with graphics. Once I felt that my profile was complete, I started my quest. My first couple of friend requests were bold—people I knew my parents wouldn't want me to talk to. I was curious, so I clicked *Add*. When I was looking at other people's profiles, I was looking to see parts of myself there. I would click on some profiles that were too sexy. Some profiles that seemed shallow. Others seemed outright fake. Some profiles seemed just right. If someone liked the same music I did, I connected. If a boy looked like he was tall, dark, and handsome, I connected.

As my courage started dying down, what my parents would

accept in a man came into full focus. I should probably find a guy online that my parents would approve of. What if we fell in love? I started to narrow my search and only connect with people my parents would approve of. Not sure why I did that. I started requesting Indian boys around Baltimore County. If he looked tall, dark, and handsome, I connected. After several requests, I decided it was time to go to sleep. In bed that night, I felt fearless and like a badass. The purpose of my Myspace profile was to look for a connection—to find anyone who could make me feel like I wasn't alone. Who also had South Asian parents and were living in an American world like me.

The first thing I did the next morning was check my profile, and I saw that a few dozen people accepted. One person caught my eye. Not only did he connect, but he also sent me a personal message thanking me for the connection and sent me a tongue face. I looked at his profile again; he was cute. He was wearing a snapback in his profile, and he also listened to rap music. I responded and told him we could talk on AOL instant messenger (AIM) and sent him my screen name. Then, I waited for him to find me and connect with me. Feeling butterflies in my stomach, I was hoping he would accept my invitation to talk. I waited desperately for him to send a message.

A few days went by, and nothing. I thought maybe this was for the best. I had so many thoughts going through my head; I convinced myself that this was a sign that I should stop trying to talk to boys. That night, I was browsing the internet when I heard a ping. It was from him! Should I respond right away? Should I wait? I decided to stop overthinking it and do it. I replied and started to ask questions, trying to get to know him. Fast forward a few weeks of talking, and I learned that he was Indian, had strict Indian parents, liked all the same music, and even had similar taste in movies. He was funny, but above all, he would talk to me like I was a human being. It was the first time in my life where I talked to an Indian man who wasn't trying to protect me or force his ideologies on me. Talking to him was fun, and I enjoyed it. Before I even realized it, I started to develop a friendship with a boy I met over the internet.

AFRAID TO LOVE

THAT SUMMER, ALL I DID WAS TALK TO HIM. WE WOULD watch movies together online. We would research stuff on the internet together. I started to know his daily activities, and he, mine. He made me smile, and I wasn't thinking anymore. One night, I woke up with a sudden realization.

Oh my God, I think I like a boy. Holy crap! What do I do? Does that mean he's going to ask me out? I'm going to be his girlfriend? I can't believe I like a boy. My parents are going to find out! I need to fly under the radar. But he's Indian. Maybe they'll be okay with it. Don't be silly, Sabreet. He's not Punjabi; you are royally screwed. It's okay, I can stop talking to him. It's never going to work. But I like him now, maybe even love him. I can't imagine a life where he's not my friend. AHHH, WHAT DO I DO?!

I had started falling for my internet crush, and now, I was having a major breakdown. There were a few reasons why I was freaking out, but the biggest was that he didn't fit into my marriage checklist. What is the marriage checklist? It's this imaginary checklist a South Asian has in their mind about the type of person they plan on marrying one day. My marriage checklist was influenced by what was and was not expected of me as a Punjabi daughter. The marriage checklist is a set of yes-and-no questions that need to be *all* yes for a person to be acceptable to introduce to your parents.

My marriage checklist:

- ☐ Is he the same race?
- ☐ The same religion?
- ☐ The same caste? Come from a good family?
- ☐ The same level of education?
- ☐ Where does he live? Can't live in India—must be American or reside in America.

My biggest problem was that my crush wasn't the same religion as me. My crush was a South Indian Hindu, and I am North Indian Sikh. Since he was a different religion, he had a different caste system, and so the question "The same caste? Come from a good family?" became obsolete. I was worried about colorism too. Colorism is real in India. North and South Indians don't intermingle with each other for a lot of reasons, but one of the cruelest reasons is that anyone who is "dark" is considered undesirable. People from the North are known to be fairer than the South. What if my family didn't want me to be with a South Indian? I decided that I was overcomplicating a simple crush. As a South Asian, it is almost in my blood to be results-driven. I was picturing being *married* to a man I just met. Since I already saw problems in marrying him, I decided it was best I take it one step at a time—who knew if this would even work? I didn't even know if he *liked* me. All I knew was that I liked him, and if he liked me back, we could maybe see where it went.

By the end of the summer, we were boyfriend and girlfriend. The first time we met each other was at Towson Mall, and he was a dream come true. He was tall and handsome and had the sweetest smile. When he saw me coming down the escalators, his mouth literally dropped, and he was covering his grin with his hand. It gave me the biggest butterflies I had ever experienced in my life. Seeing him for the first time was indescribable. It wasn't a picture that I was looking at; it was really him. A real person who understood me and who had shared similar life experiences. It's not like I could FaceTime him whenever I wanted; this was the early 2000s. Seeing him for the first time, all I wanted to do was soak in his presence for as long as I could.

When I saw him, I told him that we could only meet for, like, ten minutes because I told my mom I wanted to check out Claire's. We sat on the bench, hugged, talked for a bit, and I left within ten minutes. I didn't know when I was going to get to see him again. All I knew was that, in that moment, I knew that I wanted to be with him forever. My mind raced on the drive back home. Even though I could hide the fact that I had a boyfriend from my mother, I couldn't hide the smile he gave me.

SOUTH ASIAN SEXISM 2.0

MY MOTHER KNEW SOMETHING WAS UP WITH ME. I thought I was getting away with having a real-life boyfriend, but that was far from the truth. Since my father spent most of his time on the truck, my mother became both parents. She was vigilant and made sure I was on the right path to prosperity. The past summer, she started to notice that I had extreme emotions. I was either very happy or very sad. She noticed that I spent all my time in my room on the computer studying—which became a little suspicious. She did what she knew best; she told my little brother to keep a closer eye on me in school.

Being told to keep an eye on his older sister didn't make sense to my younger brother, but he knew why he had to do it. South Asian brothers are taught early in life to protect their younger and older sisters through a festival called Raksha Bandhan, a South Asian ceremony that celebrates the bond between sisters and brothers. Each year, sisters tie a rakhi (a red thread) on their brothers' wrist, and their brothers give them a symbolic gift of protection and a physical gift of South Asian sweets or money. Early on in their lives, the daughters are taught weakness, and the sons are taught to protect and honor their sisters. So, when it was time for my brother to protect me from a possible evil force, of course, he was all in, even if it didn't feel right.

I had no idea that I started my sophomore year with an undercover cop. My brother had also placed into Eastern, and we now went to the same school. I would avoid him in the hallway because he would always sneak up on me to see who I was hanging out with. It was at this moment that I noticed the love that my family had for me had started to change as I grew into a woman. They now had more responsibilities when it came to raising me. Overnight, I gained another parent (my brother), and I was constantly on edge trying to keep my secret American identity, friendships, and now a boyfriend from my family. The silver lining here was that my boyfriend understood me because of our South Asian connection. He didn't want his parents to know he had a girlfriend either, so we kept our relationship hidden for as long as possible. Until one day, my brother caught me.

When my brother found out that I had a secret boyfriend by looking at my Myspace account because I was dumb enough to change my relationship status to Taken," I got in trouble. Not just a little, but a lot of trouble. All my rights were instantly taken away, and I was marginalized in my family because of my gender. Again. I wasn't their child anymore; I was only their daughter. Because I was a daughter, I couldn't date. Because I was a daughter, I should know better. Because I was a daughter, my family's honor depended on my character. Because of my gender, I had to be protected and controlled. Love was a distraction, and there was no way in hell that my family was going to let that happen. My parents worked too hard for any distraction to sabotage me. Truth is, I felt ashamed to be their daughter. I didn't know why everything in my life revolved around my gender. My family made me feel like I needed so much protection. I felt weak because of my gender; they made me feel fragile. I felt that anyone could hurt me because of the societal norms that were given to me at birth.

The South Asian community is sexist. Women are silenced, and there is literature to support it. A small portion of the South Asian population is now waking up and realizing that sexism is wrong, but most of the population is still sexist, especially in the immigrant community. My parents romanticized India—the culture that India had and what India was like when they left. They didn't realize that India was changing, and that culture was changing too. This fantasy of beliefs become their identity, like a mental time machine to their past life before America. Sure, my parents let me do more than the average Punjabi girl. To even be able to wear form-fitting clothes showed how liberal my parents were, but their overall values on dating were the same. Dating wasn't allowed. A suitor would be picked for me after I got educated. I couldn't fall in love. People in our community don't fall in love. You must be focused and worry about your career. *And if, for some weird reason, you break our trust by having a boyfriend, all of your rights to get educated and become something will be taken away instantly.*

I was living in my nightmare. My parents lost faith in my ability to achieve the American dream because I fell in love. I had showed my parents that I was human; I had displayed weakness. Since I showed weakness, I now had to fight to continue school. My father mentioned that I was sixteen years old, and in another two years, I could legally get married in America. Horrified by the words that came out of his mouth, my mother shut that idea down and reminded him of the importance of education. They didn't have me in America to give me the same fate that the girls have back in India.

I managed to make the biggest mistake of my life by talking to a boy. *Why was it such a big deal that I liked and dated a boy? Why did my parents think I wasn't smart enough to make my own decisions?* My aspiration to become something didn't change because I fell in love. If anything, I felt driven to be the most successful person I knew, so I could marry him one day (if our relationship even made it that far). I had dreams that shouldn't be taken away because I allowed myself to feel. To show that you have feelings is the biggest outward expression of failure that a child of South Asian immigrant descent can show their parents. And that's exactly what I did.

Being a daughter of immigrant parents is hard. It's feeling South Asian sexism but in a redefined way—South Asian Sexism 2.0. It is a feeling of being fragile because you're a girl. You're in constant need of protection *by* the men in your family and *from* the men in society because of your beauty. In a country where other races can find me attractive, I have more eyes on me to distract me from success. It's being told dating is a distraction from success, and a suitor will be presented to you after you achieve professional success. It's being told your sexuality and reproductive health don't matter; your silence matters. It's being told self-love doesn't exist; only complete devotion to your parents and their dreams exists. I was defined by the roles and obligations other people bestowed on me before I could even begin to understand who I wanted to be. As a daughter, every decision I made needed to be approved. Especially now, because I had broken my parents' trust by showing them the worst kind of betrayal there is: talking to a man who wasn't my husband.

HIDDEN PAIN

AS HER YOUNGER BROTHER, IT WAS HARD TO SEE THE PHYSICAL and emotional damage he had caused his family. He had done what he was told to do, but that didn't mean that it didn't hurt him. It hurt to see his family this way. It hurt a little more to see his sister this way. She was his best friend—even if he didn't want to admit it now because they were both teenagers. He grew up playing outside with her, going to the library with her, experiencing every family moment with her. She lived every single experience he had so far in his life with him, and for that, he loved her. More than he understood. It's because he loved her so much that he didn't understand why things had to be different in raising her. Why he had to protect her. Why things had to be harder on him because everyone was so fascinated with protecting her when she didn't even need it. His sister was the biggest badass he had ever met. He never worried about her if she was alone. She could really take care of herself; she took care of him when he was scared. She was strong, spoke her mind, and was driven not to take nonsense from anyone. She'd always been that way, for as long as he could remember. To be the source of why she was unhappy now caused him pain. Even though it didn't make any sense, he rationalized the decision he had to make by telling himself that his parents knew what was best for her, even though he was pretty sure he knew better.

* * *

My mother was fighting her own battles. Not only did she start hiding things she caught me doing from my father, but she also started putting her marriage in jeopardy by doing this. She blamed her working schedule for not guiding me. She thought it was because of her shortcomings that I somehow fell in love. She became depressed because she didn't want the opportunities that she had wished for taken away from her daughter because she was a teenage girl in America. She didn't blame her for liking a boy. She blamed the South Asian community and its inability to change. She was aware that being in a different country meant that her children would grow up differently, but she never expected a challenge like this: having to deal with a husband who was still traditional in his thinking about how to raise children in America; dealing with a community looking for a good juicy story about her family. All children make mistakes. What made all the difference was that her daughter had made the ultimate mistake—caring for her heart first. She didn't want her to grow up compromising her desires. My mother had lived her whole life compromising what she wanted because she wasn't strong enough to voice her own mind in the South Asian community. Whenever she did, she was met with an altercation in her marriage. As soon as she became a mother, she willingly set her desires aside to let her children dream. She wanted her daughter to be the most outspoken woman in the world. She wanted her to learn from her mistakes and fight for herself. Scared for her daughter's future, she did the next best thing she could to ease her mind and protect her child: she prayed that God would give her strength and bring her back on the right path.

* * *

The truth is that his identity was changing too. He had started to feel that some of the beliefs of the South Asian culture about women were wrong. He didn't want his daughter to be a victim of sexism. She was so much more than that. To think that he was expected to raise her only to have her be a slave to another family—he could not accept that was the only value she could provide to this world. The painful truth is he didn't feel prepared to raise her here from the moment she was born. He loved her with all his heart but raising her brought out demons he couldn't control. He saw so much of himself in her. To see the impact his words were having on her was hard. It hurt him. He had seen more life than her. He had known more men than her. He knew what men were after, especially at this age. He didn't want to picture his daughter all grown up. She was still that little kid who loved ice cream. When did she grow up? If he didn't show her what it meant to not get educated and to be stupid in love, she would regret her choices for the rest of her life. She would believe that she was nothing more than a body.

Seeing her fall in love so early also made him afraid. He feared she had lost sight of what it meant to be successful. He wanted her to know that he didn't want to destroy her life. That it was okay to fall in love; just not now. Maybe after she had a career? If he let her know he was okay with her having a love marriage now, would she lose her drive? Would she get educated? There's one thing he knew well: having someone underestimate your potential drives you crazy. It makes you want to prove them wrong. It fuels your desire to be successful. His parents did that to him, and look where he landed. He was ok with having his daughter hate him. He hated himself right now too. He didn't understand what he did wrong to make her be so careless and fall in love. He couldn't help that he felt like she didn't care about his struggle. Didn't care that he was driving day and night to provide for her and her brother. It hurt him. All he did was think about them. Why wasn't she thinking about him when she started talking to this boy? Was he so insignificant in her life that she completely disregarded him? He already felt insignificant driving aimlessly as a truck driver across America. But having his family think he was insignificant hurt. He couldn't shake the feeling of betrayal that came with knowing that, for a brief second, her father didn't matter to her.

ENOUGH

I WAS HAVING A DIFFICULT TIME FEELING ACCEPTED IN high school in my junior year. Feeling unwanted by my family drove me to a depressed state. I had nobody to turn to. I couldn't get on the computer anymore, and if I did, I was monitored. I couldn't talk to my boyfriend, which led to us breaking up. I was alone, unsupported, and in desperate need of love and attention from anyone. I started to withdraw from my studies. My grades dropped. I genuinely didn't care where my life was going. The biggest reason was that I didn't feel like I could be that smart, modest, Indian daughter my parents so desperately wanted me to be.

At the age of sixteen, I felt like I already made the biggest mistake of my life, so now, what was the point of living? Even if I became successful and I could marry a man I wanted, what would be the chances that my first love would still wait for me? What were the chances I would even get to marry someone I like? My parents were strict. I started hiding my academic failure. I let the people around me define my potential. I was depressed and alone, and I didn't see why this life was worth living.

Noticing how much I had changed, my mother decided to step in and try a different tactic to understand me. She decided that she was going to be my friend because she saw that I had nobody to turn to. My mom approached me to show me how fortunate I was, even in my misfortune.

Mom: *Sabreet, you have the freedom to be who you want to be because you are American. Do you have any idea how lucky you are? Even though you are American, you must put a box around you to show us that you understand the Indian culture. If you don't want to be honest with us, that's okay; hide it. You must understand we want the best for you, but you have to want the best for you too. Why are you giving up on life?*

Me: *Because there is no point, I'm bad. Nothing I can do will ever make you or Papa see that on the inside, I'm a good person.*

Mom: *You are not bad.*

Me: *Yes, I am.*

Mom: *Sabi, no. Listen, I am here for you. My daughter will not be helpless. Just because you are a woman, people treat you differently in our community. That's okay. You must fight the game and play it to win. How are you going to win and be what you want to be by letting people get to you? You are smarter than that. If someone says you're bad, that doesn't make you bad. If someone thinks you're bad, show them what makes you good. The only way people will respect a woman in our community is if she is educated. You must be educated, Sabi. Your whole life depends on it. You've only lived a short amount of life so far. If you don't get educated now, people will make you become what they want you to be. A body with no voice. Education will give you a voice, don't give up on yourself. I'm not giving up on you. You can do it. Keep failing, and I'll keep pushing you. I'm your mother, and that will never change. I want to make you something, God damnit.*

Even though I didn't see it then, my mom did get me. She was right—I needed to play the game. If I wanted to have my own freedom, my own rights, and my own voice, I needed to play the damn game. I didn't have to play the game against *her*; she understood, for the most part. But my father was very traditional and couldn't see the value I provided to him anymore. Playing the game is a lot easier said than done with him. I had already started seeing violence when I didn't obey and had to do household chores (like make tea, clean, and feed my brother) at all hours of the day. If I voiced that I didn't want to do something, I was met with a belittling encounter.

Why are you talking back? How dare you? What respect do we have in the community now? We don't even know if people know you had a boyfriend. Women are to do what they are told.

Any whisper under my breath, breathing too loudly, or being too slow to respond set my father off. I learned to walk on eggshells and stay quiet, so I could prove to him that I was not the lowlife he thought I was.

My mother was my hidden supporter. Like she said, women don't have a voice in our community, and she didn't have one. My mother kept me strong when everyone left me. My friends at school left me because I was always unhappy. My boyfriend couldn't talk to me anymore, so he had to leave me. My family left me. But she didn't leave me. She was right there. She became a friend who was honest and tried to show me how to get the hell out of the sexist culture I was in because she understood what it meant to be a woman.

Feeling suppressed and powerless was one of the hardest things I have ever had to deal with in my life. Especially as a teenager when life is already overly emotional. There were days where the fantasy of what my life could be (if I persevered through this madness) versus my current reality was too much for me to handle. Even though I didn't have freedom, I had my music. I would take my CD player to the only place in my house where I could have privacy—the bathroom. I would cry for as long as possible until someone told me to get out. The bathroom became my therapist's office, and my CD player became my therapist. There were days when the bathroom brought out the darkest, deepest emotions in me to the extent that I would harm myself. My mother and brother would try to open the door and tell me that it would be okay; I had to believe. But it was hard to believe. Even though I loved my boyfriend, I couldn't be with him. I knew he loved me too. He would reach out to a mutual friend to ask how I was doing and if I was okay. I couldn't shake this feeling that we were supposed to be together forever. I'd never connected with anyone that deeply before. Unsure if I was stupid in love or if this was meant to be, I had to ignore my agony and try to move on.

It was hard to move on, so my mother reminded me that women are brave. The only weakness we will ever have in ourselves is thinking we are not enough. We were born enough. Time and time again, we are born with more than enough. *The world will show us again and again that we are not enough, but you must ignore the world and focus on who you truly are on the inside.* My worth wasn't determined the day the picture of Guru Nanak Dev Ji came down in our apartment. It wasn't determined the day I came home without *Congratulations* balloons. My worth will always be determined by what I do with the challenges given to me since birth. To overcome an obstacle requires the same bravery that I was born with. Sometimes, that bravery comes in small realizations of your potential. Because of my mother's faith in me then, I am able to write this book now. I had to remind myself that I was enough, and I started to figure out how to fix my high school transcript and bring it back to the state it was in before I fell in love.

HAPPILY NEVER
AFTER

I BROUGHT MY GRADES UP IN HIGH SCHOOL, BUT ONE BAD semester had done enough damage to last a lifetime. How was I going to get into college when I had less than ideal grades on my transcript? I convinced myself that no college was going to accept me because I had a few bad grades. I was so convinced and afraid of failing that I didn't even take the SATs. To make matters worse, the kids in my high school thought I was some sort of a rebel when I wasn't.

In truth, it didn't matter what people thought about me (at home or at school). What mattered was that I was a first-generation Indian American. The first in my family to go to school in America. I needed to be the first in my family to get accepted into and graduate from college. I devised a plan that would ensure I got into college, and I put my whole heart into it. If you put your heart and soul into something, you always succeed. There wasn't a waking moment where I didn't chase after my dream of going to a community college and turning my grades upside down. Not only did I get accepted into the half-day community college program in high school, but I started to get back some of the trust I had lost from my family. I wanted to show them that I was taking school seriously and that I was really trying to change my life.

To get my parents to trust me again, I had to tell them that the biggest mistake of my life was falling in love with a boy. Even though falling in love was one of the best things that had ever happened to me, it wasn't to them, and they needed to hear their reality through me for us to fully move on. I was comfortable lying to my parents because they wanted to be comforted in a lie instead of understanding my truth then. Losing your voice and feeling powerless teaches you the importance of *having* a voice, your own voice. Even though it was going to take a long time for me to fully let my inner voice shine, I was censoring my truth to be accepted by my family. Censoring my truth became my reality well into my adulthood because I was a daughter. The real truth was I still loved my ex-boyfriend, but we decided, in order to honor my parents, it was best for us to maintain a friendship and put our full efforts into trying to pursue the dreams our parents had for us—to get educated.

Getting caught with a boy drove me to want to be the most successful woman I could be. There was a certain level of certainty that I felt with him. Everything in my mind, body, and soul told me this wasn't the first time I met him. I felt like I had known him for a million lifetimes. I knew we were meant to be together forever. I couldn't stop loving him even if I wasn't allowed to. I remember the last phone call we had. He promised me he would always love me. He told me that no matter what, if we were meant to be, we would be. Nobody could stop it. He told me to be the smartest girl my parents had ever seen. He didn't say, "Bye"; he told me he would see me later. He promised me that if I held up my end of the deal (be confident and be the smart girl he knew I could be), he would keep his end of the deal (be the smartest Indian I knew he could be) because we both had to be smart for our parents. He gave me a fantasy that one day when we were old, we would be sipping on lemonade, swinging on a porch swing in our front yard, watching the sunset, holding hands, and thinking about the long life we had lived together. It's just that life was giving us lemons right now, and we would make our lemonade together later in life. Every victory I had, I found a way to tell him—even if it was through a prepaid phone call or through a mutual friend we had. He celebrated every single one of my victories. When he got into college, I knew and celebrated silently, alone. Silence became our relationship; it became our constant. My faith in our relationship was so strong that it continued to fuel my fire and push me, even when I didn't have it in me to continue.

Part VII

EARNING
THE DREAM

MONEY'S WORTH

I WAS ABLE TO TAKE FOUR COLLEGE CLASSES WHILE I WAS in high school, which led me to kick-start my college degree. I took summer classes and started my first official fall semester at the Community College of Baltimore County with eighteen credits. I decided to take nine classes and had gotten special permission from the academic advisors. I stressed to them that I have nothing else on my plate—I was only here to study, and I genuinely meant it. Going to a community college for my first year of college was a no-brainer.

My tuition and books at a community college cost a fraction of what it would have in a traditional state university. Still, even though tuition was cheaper, it didn't mean it wasn't expensive for us. Even though my parents were blue-collar workers, I didn't qualify for income-based financial aid because my parents were making more than the Federal Poverty Level (FPL) allowed. What did that mean exactly? It meant that my family was the in-between. We weren't poor enough to receive assistance but didn't have the financial ability to pay for college tuition because we were living paycheck to paycheck. My parents didn't have money stored away for their future, like typical South Asian parents. They were helping us by providing us with necessities. That's all they could provide, and that was okay. Unfortunately, regardless of our financial situation, I still had to figure out a way to pay my tuition, which felt impossible. I was under eighteen and my life of credit didn't exist yet. The money had to come from somewhere; I just didn't know where.

The only way I could pay my tuition was with my mother's paychecks. I told my mother at the beginning of the summer that I would need to pay money for my fall tuition. Even though it was on the top of my mind, it was not on the top of her mind. It was the final week before my tuition was due. If I didn't pay it, my seat would be vacated, and I couldn't attend the semester. My mother told me that we could go when she got paid on Friday. She got paid $987 for two weeks of work at McDonald's. I was about to use 99.9 percent of her check to pay for my tuition. That didn't cover the cost of my books, her car bill, or our living expenses. She told me she would borrow money from a friend to cover her bills until her next paycheck. Watching my mother hand over her check to me—a check she worked day and night to earn—killed me. I think a piece of me died that day, realizing that no matter how hard you work, life can be unfair. My mother believed so strongly in my dreams that she didn't bat an eye and handed over her check that took her two weeks to earn. I saw the physical toll working at McDonald's had on her body. Yet she showed me strength, kindness, and unwavering faith in my dreams. When I went to the Bursar's Office, I handed in the check my mom postdated so that the money could be in her account in time for it to be cleared. The clerk noticed but didn't say anything. She handed me the receipt, and I held on to it. This was living proof of my mother's struggle, and it was not going to go in vain. I kept that receipt and looked at it several times throughout my semester.

BLUE-COLLAR ILLUSION

HAVING A STRAIGHT-*A* AVERAGE, I FELT THAT I WAS GOOD enough to apply to our state school—the University of Maryland College Park. In community college, I learned what I was passionate about and what came naturally to me: sociology. I majored in sociology because it was the study of society, and I was fascinated by it. How people think and why has always intrigued me. I decided that if I majored in sociology, I was going to get my PhD one day because I loved research. I wanted to understand all the ins and outs of society and research everything I possibly could to do that. After carefully tailoring my application to the sociology department, I submitted my application, along with my college transcript and three letters of recommendation. Within two months, I heard back and learned that I was accepted into one of the best four-year schools in Maryland. Even though I was happy that I got accepted, I started to worry about the details of my acceptance.

How am I going to pay for college when my parents cannot afford to pay for my tuition? Would financial aid help me? My brother is going there next year too. How are my parents going to afford two children in college?

I didn't know where to turn, and I was scared. Figuring out how to pay for a college education is hard. An advisor told me that I could apply for FAFSA to see if I qualified for a student loan. FAFSA is a form you can use to apply for a loan from the federal government to help pay for your tuition expenses. I had no idea that I qualified for a loan like that. If I took the loan, I would have to pay it back six months after I graduated or pay monthly installments until the loan was paid off. That sounded like a long time, and I felt confident that if I went to college and graduated, I would have a job that I could use to pay off my loan. I felt like it was too good to be true. I looked to see if there were any catches. As an eighteen-year-old, I didn't see any. I made the decision to apply and accepted the loan on my own because I was the only literate person in my family. Getting student loans was the only option I had. It truly felt like a benefit I was receiving because I lived in America. I lived in a country that could offer me my dream of getting educated. As there was no doubt in my mind that I would be successful enough to pay off my student loans, I signed the dotted line and sealed the first financial coffin of my adult life.

The summer before college, I looked for a job to help me save up money. After weeks of looking, my parents finally let me work at a McDonald's because my mother knew the staff there. I didn't care where it was; I was happy I had a job that could help me prepare for my future. My parents didn't have to tell me that they didn't have enough money to support and buy college supplies for both of their children. I just knew that they couldn't afford it. I wanted to save enough money to buy my own laptop and pay my rent at school.

My first job at McDonald's taught me the importance of being resilient. Seeing how my favorite meals were cooked and how quickly the staff worked to make sure we delivered what customers ordered was exhilarating. I was making money and working a job that allowed me to have a summer break when I got off work. The only aspect that was hard about my job was the costumers. Since I was a dining room cashier, I saw it all. People were rude and sometimes downright evil. If someone messed up the order in the back, I became the punching bag.

Do you not speak English?! Why did you mess up my order? Go back to your country. America is for Americans, Hindu. Because of people like you, I pay more in taxes. If you don't know how to work the cash register, get on food stamps. That's what everyone who doesn't want to work hard enough does, and you, you're barely working.

The hardest part was that I had to smile and let them think they were right, even if what they said was far from the truth. In food services, you have no voice. Even if people are treating you poorly, the customer is always right, no matter what. Every time someone told me I was a foreigner, I wanted to scream out how American I was. Every time someone told me to go back to my country, I wanted to say, "Oh, so like go back to New York?" Every comment that was said to me, I responded in my mind with the answer I wanted to say, but the only words that ever came out of my mouth were, "I am sorry, let me fix that for you." I kept quiet, no matter how angry I became on the inside because I needed this job. I wanted to shout at the top of my voice, "I'm a college student! I have potential! I'm going to the University of Maryland, College Park." Screaming that would not only have gotten me fired, but it would have undermined the hardworking people I worked with every day. It would have meant that I thought I was better than my own parents, and I was not.

I knew working a labor job was hard physical work, but I didn't account for how mentally exhausting it was. Poor people undermine their intelligence, no matter how smart they are, because they are forced to be quiet. They stay quiet because they need the money, but I didn't realize then was that my labor job was preparing me for my first semester at College Park. Being mentally and physically exhausted is the reality of every college student in America today.

EMANCIPATED

FREEDOM. EVERY STUDENT WHO HAS LIVED ON CAMPUS has experienced exactly what I'm talking about. If you come from a strict family, living on campus can feel like you got pardoned from a life sentence. This new freedom hits you like an ocean and then continues to hit you like waves as you try to discover who you are. I realized I was free at college when I didn't have to explain my whereabouts to anyone. I could get up and leave whenever I wanted. Go anywhere I wanted. I didn't have to tell anyone where I was going or why. I could just go. That feeling changed my life. So much so that I went off the rails, and I lost balance. I tried to stay the course, but it was hard when the temptations of having something you've never had before were right there in front of you every single day. To quote Spiderman, "With great power comes great responsibility," and I was learning just how great that responsibility could be.

Learning how to properly study for college should be taught to you somewhere in your journey through the public-school system. When I got to a real college and was given freedom and then told to study, I struggled hard. I didn't know how to balance my hard courses with my easier courses. I had to learn how to balance my free time with studying and having fun; it was harder than I expected. The problem is that freedom is complicated.

I finally had a chance to define my own priorities on my own terms, but I was overshadowed by guilt because I was back in a romantic relationship with the same boy I met on Myspace, who was also at College Park. Even though studying occupied most of my time, how I spent my free time bothered me. I spent all my time with him because it was the first time in my life that I could. When I spent time with him, I felt ashamed. I knew it was okay to spend time with someone you loved; but I still felt uneasy. I was not emotionally mature enough to understand why and what I should do about it.

Having the freedom to choose what to do with my time and trying not to feel like I was betraying my parents' trust was the foundation of my guilt as an adult in college. Love is hard for a South Asian woman. In the South Asian culture, love is defined as an obligation or a responsibility that is bestowed on you. It's never something that is just given to you because of who you are; it's always earned through merit. So, naturally, I became confused when my boyfriend loved me genuinely and purely without asking for anything in return. Unable to process his love, I let that shame turn into doubt. That doubt into fear. That fear into believing I wasn't enough to be loved. Not just by him, but by anyone. I had convinced myself that I wasn't smart or worthy of love. I didn't know how to process my emotional state of mind when all I needed was clarity to study.

I spent most of my time in college struggling to balance my professional and free time. I felt like, regardless of how hard I tried, I wasn't getting the As I was used to. I was average, and being average is the worst thing to be when the pressure to become something great has never been more intense. College is exhausting. It requires a certain amount of rigorous control over yourself to achieve something that you can't see immediately. Children of immigrant parents go to college alone because they learn how to fight the hardest battles alone from the beginning.

As a brown child, you never tell your parents if you are struggling. Especially when you don't feel like that "Smart Indian," there is this enormous amount of guilt you feel that you are failing to perform at your highest level for your parents.

Oversleeping your 8:00 a.m. class, getting that C in calculus, and simply not being able to focus on your work makes you feel guiltier than you have ever felt in your life. I felt guilty because I knew, deep down inside, my life was easier than my parents'. Yet here I was, taking the comfortable life they had given me and not working towards what was expected of me.

What's wrong with me? How was this fair to my parents, who are working overtime trying to educate me?

This guilt of being average consumed my mental health, day in and day out. I felt depressed. I turned to anything to make me feel better, whether that was alcohol or watching shows I probably shouldn't have been watching in the first place. I felt that sadness every single day. Even if I experienced a small victory, guilt was the only emotion that I knew how to feel. I felt ashamed that I had an easier life than my parents because I had been given the opportunity to get an education, and I was constantly remorseful for choosing to be in a romantic relationship as a South Asian woman. Even though going to college emancipated me from my family, I handcuffed my self-worth around the guilt and shame I felt for leaving them in the first place.

ALIENATION

MY FIRST INTERACTION WITH A BROWN STUDENT IN ONE of my classes was a bit strange.

Student: *Oh, so you're a first-generation American?*

Me: *Yeah, what about you?*

Student: *My dad was born here, so I think I'm second generation. What do your parents do?*

Me: *They own a business.*

Student: *Mine too; my dad has his own law firm.*

Me: *Cool.*

Awkward silence. I looked away to show I wasn't interested in continuing the conversation. The student looked uncomfortable.

Student: *Okay, I'll see you around.*

I found myself becoming cold towards other South Asians

because most of them were, in fact, "Smart Indians." Here I was, wishing to be at the finish line, while at the same time, that very line I wanted to cross was their starting point. I desperately wanted to avoid anyone who didn't understand where I came from. I wanted nothing more than to come from a family with professional jobs. While desperately searching for meaning, I isolated myself from my own culture, even though I wanted nothing more than to belong to something.

When I first joined UMD, I thought maybe I could find people like me. UMD has a big South Asian student community; I even joined a South Asian sorority, so I could make brown friends. But I found that I was afraid of making new friends. I was afraid of interacting with everyone because I thought everyone came from some sort of privilege that I didn't have. Afraid of being rejected, I didn't go out of my way to meet anyone outside of my roommates or my boyfriend's friends, and I felt like I wasn't getting the full college experience. I was afraid of being exposed because I didn't want everyone to see the real me. They always say that you are supposed to find your people in college, and yet I was struggling hard to find anyone who I felt like I could relate to.

Along with struggling to find friends, I also struggled with what values I wanted to uphold and what values I felt were too traditional. I started hanging out exclusively with brown students to feel a sense of acceptance and normalcy. The more I hung out with them, the more I realized that even though we looked the same, I still didn't fit in with them. Some kids were too modern for me. They didn't want to live with their parents after college. They didn't think about their parents at all. They were thinking about themselves and their happiness only. I genuinely didn't understand. *How could you be a brown student and not worry about your parents?*

During this phase of my life, I noticed another disadvantage of not being that "Smart Indian." It meant that my whole identity was tied to giving back to my parents—to provide for them whatever they had provided for me. For other kids, their parents had their lives already figured out. They had savings. They had businesses. They had everything—or at least, that's what I thought from the outside looking in. The difference between them and me? They were in college trying to find a career that could make their parents happy; they were not worried about how to support them later in life. I was in college trying to find a career that would make my parents' sacrifice worth it by being successful. Success was defined by finding an occupation that could not only take care of me but of them too.

Honestly, it was my duty, and I was proud to uphold that traditional view of taking care of your parents, but it came at a price. Imagine filtering yourself and trying to build true friendships based on that filter in college. It's impossible. I was never truly honest about my family. How traditional things were for me. It's hard to start a friendship with people when you're not honest with them. I kept everyone at arm's length and would internalize my depression when I realized that maybe I wasn't going to find those South Asian people I had been looking for in college either.

TIRELESS DEDICATION

THE MONEY THAT I SAVED UP FROM MY SUMMER JOB AT McDonald's didn't last long. After the third month of my freshmen year, I had to ask my parents to help me, even though I was well aware they were struggling. They had their mortgage to pay for, everything for the trucking company, their household bills, and money for my brother's room and board. Since I shared a room, my rent was $425 a month. I knew there was no way they could afford this additional burden, and I had tried to find a way to pay for myself. I told them not to worry about me, but I had failed. That failure immobilized me.

I missed my parents, so I went back home one weekend to hang out with them. That weekend, I started to see the true reality of what was happening while my brother and I were away at college. My mom was barely eating, so she could send us money to eat at school. Since my dad lived in the truck, driving from place to place, he was gone for weeks at a time, leaving my mom completely alone at home. I could see the physical toll of the battles she was hiding in her heart. But she never let me know. She asked how school was and if there was anything she could help me with.

When I was about to head back to College Park, my mom suggested that since my dad was driving his truck to a truck stop halfway from home to college, it would be a good idea to ride with him. I agreed. It was the first time in a long time that I was having fun with my dad. He was joking around with me and telling me jokes about all the stupid drivers on the road that tried to cut him off. After some time, he got a bit quiet, and I asked him what was on his mind.

Papa: *Nothing.*

Me: *No, it's something. What are you thinking about?*

Papa: *Well, Sabi, this might come as a surprise to you, but I think you are mature and wiser than your brother.*

Me: *What?*

Papa: *What I'm saying is you understand more than your brother. You feel more. You can sense more.*

Me: *Papa, I don't know what you are talking about.*

I was deeply panicking that he somehow knew about my boyfriend.

Papa: *Sabi, I'm saying…we need help. Your mother and I—we can't afford both you and your brother in college at the same time. Getting a job over the summer really helped us. Is there any way you could find a job that can cover your expenses in college? We are trying to put you and your brother through school, and I don't think we can do it alone.*

Me: *Papa, yes, sure, I can try. Don't worry; I'll figure it out.*

I realized that this was the first time my dad had talked to me as an adult.

Papa: *I've been thinking about it a lot, and I didn't want to ask you. I've been praying for God to show me a way, especially when we are so close to making you both something, but I can't see the way. I know Waheguru will take care of my family and me. He always has.*

Me: *Papa, don't worry. I got it.*

Papa: *But I don't want you working any job, Sabi. Can you find an interview that you can use for your career? If you work a labor job now, you will get beaten down by the hardship that comes with it, and I want to make sure the job you find will help your career in the long run. Can you try for me? Sorry for asking this of you. I know it's hard, and jobs aren't easy to find. But I have no other choice.*

His voice was starting to sound funny, and he wasn't looking at me anymore.

Me: (turning back to him) *Papa, don't worry, I got this.*

As soon as I got back to my dorm, I started crying uncontrollably. I didn't know what to do. It broke my heart to hear my dad in such pain. I felt alone, confused, and helpless. In my desperation, there was one thing I knew for sure: I was all I needed. I got this. I needed to find my own way to pay for school. Unable to sleep that night, I looked up every possible job I could apply to, and I applied to every single one of them. The local bookstore, BookHolders was hiring an immediate position; all you had to do was fill out the application and come in person. The next morning, I decided to skip my 9:30 a.m. lab and see if I could get that job. I showed up, handed them my application, and indicated that I was eager to work whenever and however they needed. Lucky for me, they were always busy and needed bodies. I was hired, and I felt instantly relieved because I could help my parents with their burden.

While I was too busy trying to figure out all the *ins* and *outs* of college, my mother was living her own secret life. She had lost her job. To help out, she supported my dad so he could make even more money on the truck. She became his dispatch (kind of like a trucking secretary) to help ease the burden. It's hard going from a job that gives you a sense of meaning to being a full-time, stay-at-home wife, who is now supporting her husband's blue-collar career. Even though she tried to find another job and applied everywhere, it was not easy finding a job. Especially not then.

It was extremely difficult for my mom to find a job, and she became depressed. Her depression deepened because she lived alone in the house. Both of her children weren't around; they were in college. Her husband was always on the truck and came home maybe once a month, if that. Her extended family didn't live with her anymore because they were settled now and had lives of their own. She had no one at work or at home around her—ever. She was completely isolated, and it was taking a physical toll on her body.

The only value she thought she had now was to support her family. She didn't know how to support them when the past-due bills came in. She thought it was her job to figure it out. Guilty and unsure of how to help, she refused to talk to her family members because she didn't want to take their peace away. She suffered alone, trying to pull off short-term loans from her friends to fix the problem. While I was at college trying to figure out how to go to school, work, and graduate with a job, my mom was feeling the same way I was even though our battles were a bit different. We were trying to endure the darkness in our hearts by choosing to be quiet—the thing that we knew best to do because we were women.

DROWNING IN COMMITMENT

THROUGHOUT COLLEGE, I WAS MOSTLY STAYING AFLOAT. The job at BookHolders wasn't enough to pay all my bills, so I kept applying to jobs. During my first year living away at College Park, I always had late rent notices slid under my apartment door, where I lived with three other individuals. I was always embarrassed coming home because I knew they saw my notices and would pretend like they didn't see them. If you were late paying your rent, there would be an additional fee on your account, and you had the entire month to pay both the rent and the additional fee. To me, it seemed like a justified fee because it would give my family until the end of the month to pay the rent. There was this one time where both of our collective efforts weren't enough to pay for rent, and I got an eviction notice. Stressed beyond belief, my father sold his old truck to give me enough money to cover my bills for three months. Even to this day, I have no idea how my parents afforded the cost of three living spaces each month.

It took a full year to find a job that would pay enough to cover my entire room and board costs. I somehow was able to land an internship in Washington, DC. I don't even remember applying to it because I was applying to everything. Whenever I wasn't studying, I would spend all my waking hours applying to every single job posted on the college board. All the jobs that the online college port posted were white-collar jobs. Any of these jobs seemed like a step in the right direction. Any of them would do. I needed the money.

When I got that call to be interviewed and then was told that I was selected for the job, it changed my whole life. I was going to be an intern, and they were going to start me at $13.14 an hour. I had to work at least part-time to keep my job. If I worked more, that was fine; I had to let my manager know. I had the opportunity to make the salary of a full-time employee of $27,431. Do you have any idea how much money that is for an undergrad student?! In a moment, my whole life changed. Not only was I going to be able to afford my rent and living expenses alone, but I had a little extra money to save for a rainy day for my family. The internship in DC saved my life and jump-started my professional career. The price tag it came with was my sanity.

Going to school and working full-time is excruciating. I had to cut corners somewhere to make time for everything. Those corners became my mental health and the few friendships I somehow made in college. Fall semester of 2011, I started working and going to school full-time, and my grades suffered a bit. I wasn't putting in my best effort because I was always tired.

Since I didn't have a car and I lived off-campus, I had to commute to DC every single day on the bus and the Metro to get to where I needed to go. When you depend on public transportation, you plan your whole day around when the bus/Metro is available. I took night classes, so I could go to work at 6:00 a.m. and be out by :003 p.m., so I could get to school by 5:30 p.m. for my night classes. Sometimes I missed the class because it was out of my control. The main point is, I was always rushing from one destination to the other. I was running on low sleep, trying to finish all my homework and everything else in between. It was hard.

When I wanted to wallow in self-pity, I thought about my father: *he literally lives at his job, every day, to provide for me, and I'm complaining about doing too much?* I didn't listen to my body or mind. My pain didn't exist, and it wasn't allowed to exist. Every single cry I felt from my body and my mind wasn't justified enough to be given the attention it deserved. I didn't realize it then, but ignoring these warning signs from your body can literally take your life. We are trained in the South Asian community to ignore our bodies and operate nonstop like machines. I was working and studying myself to death, so much that burn-out culture became my new professional norm.

THE AMERICAN DREAM

THE HAPPIEST MOMENT OF MY FAMILY'S AND MY LIFE WAS graduating from undergrad. Not only were we celebrating my graduation from college, we were also celebrating how I was moving on to the next phase of my life. I had gotten into grad school, and I'd even found a full-time job in Baltimore. I was the first woman in my family to graduate with a college degree in America. The moment was monumental and surreal. My mother and I got our nails done. My two best friends came from Baltimore. Everyone came to support the dream of what I had just become. I had become living, breathing proof of my parents' sacrifice. Proof that their sacrifice was worth it.

In my unstructured college experience, I had learned how to be a collection of all my experiences at once. I learned to make the land of opportunity my own, even if it was hard. I learned that freedom truly isn't free and that I love my family more than I know how to express. Everyone showed up and was ready to celebrate with me on the morning of my graduation day. Everyone was coming, except for Papa. My mother gently told me on the morning of my graduation day that Papa wouldn't be able to make it. He had tried hard to deliver his load on time, but the team that was unloading his truck was taking longer than expected, and he was four hours away from Maryland. Disappointed but understanding that he had to work, I accepted that my father would not be present on not only the biggest day of my life but also of his. His first child in America had an American education.

Before saying, "Good-bye" to my family and friends (because we had to go line up,) my mother ran over to me and told me that Papa might make it if he sped straight to the university. My father was on his way to College Park. He was going to miss the ceremony, but he was going to be there afterward to see me. Somehow, someway, he was going to be here to see what the American dream could mean. When the ceremony was over, and we were released to our families, I raced over to look for one person and one person only: my father. When I saw my father, I asked him:

Me: *What do you want to say today?! How do you feel?*

Papa: *Happy. I'm proud of you; keep it up.*

Me: *No, Papa, this is because of you. Papa, if they called you on stage, what would you say?*

Papa: *I would say that I gave my blood and soul to America. I gave America my children. That is the only thing I have that I could give to this country. America has taken care of my children and let them shine. I want to thank everyone who helped make this America possible.*

That's all he said. He thanked America for accepting us and giving us the opportunity to shine. He undermined what he had just provided for his family.

What my father couldn't see was just how much it meant to

me that he was there. He was there, and that's all that mattered. He chose not to sleep and drove straight to see me. It didn't matter to me that he hadn't showered in six days because he was driving nonstop. It didn't matter to me that he was in jeans and an oil-stained T-shirt. It didn't matter to me that he looked extremely tired. It didn't matter to me that he wasn't the most well-groomed, well-rested father of a graduate. What mattered to me was that he was there, despite all the obstacles that were thrown his way. What makes my father is his sheer will and determination to persevere, no matter what. Those are the values I want to uphold and live by for the rest of my life. I am proud to not be that "Smart Indian" because not being that "Smart Indian" means you are tough. It means you will climb out the well of hell to be there for the people you love. It means that you drive along the roads of America, trying to feed your family. My father is a truck driver, and he has made me who I am today. That is the reality of the America I live in—where a truck driver can give you the American dream. How many people can say that?

Part VIII

UNITED
BY LOVE

APOLOGETICALLY GROWN

WHEN CHILDREN OF IMMIGRANT, BLUE-COLLAR PARENTS earn a degree, it gives their parents a sense of security. Their sacrifice has paid off, and they finally have a retirement strategy: their children. The children themselves experience a newfound reality that they may not be ready for: how to be an "adult."

After I graduated, I felt like nothing had changed, but everything had changed. I now had a job that paid well, and I was going to graduate school to further my career. I was being hit with responsibilities, and I didn't know how to process my next step in life. The first stressor I experienced was figuring out how to pay back the student loans that I took out. My father stressed the importance of paying them all back by the grace period so I could start saving money. I listened to him, and I started living at home to rapidly pay off my debt.

The sheer reality that I must pay thousands of dollars as soon as possible made me feel completely lost. How is it even possible to pay back all this money immediately? How in the world was I going pay off $22,918 in student loan debt when I also had a fourteen-thousand-dollar bill to pay for graduate school? The pressure of paying for your student loans, paying for your future education, helping your parents, and trying to understand how to manage your money is extremely ruthless. Even though my parents were nowhere near financially secure, they never expected me to help them. I felt financially tied to my student loans, which made me view my parents' suffering through the sidelines as they continued to support me, even when I was an adult with a job.

I started to feel angry. I didn't know what to do to even marginally help them without burying myself in debt. How did my parents become my roots in America? How were they able to provide for me with so much security? My whole life had been a constant reminder to pull myself up by my bootstraps. My parents were so busy buying my boots that it became my responsibility to make sure our bootstraps stayed on later in life. What I didn't account for was helping my parents immediately after college because that's when they needed it the most. Even though I kept pushing and moving towards the American dream, it was at every new step I faced that I realized just how far behind we were as a family.

To further complicate my adult identity, in the South Asian community, you aren't considered an adult until you are married. The only difference between me before college and me after college was that I had a degree and a job, and I was an unmarried woman who was twenty-two years old. My mother didn't mention marriage to me; she said we could think about it after I was done with my master's. But my father started to worry where in the hell he was going to find me a nice Punjabi man to marry. Marriage was the last thing on my mind, even though I knew who I wanted to marry. Right now, I was trying to figure out how to assimilate into my dual identity again, now that I was back home from college.

Even though I was educated now, I was still a daughter. I was expected home at a certain time. I was to be respectful and modest and to realize that my parents' honor depended on how I displayed myself. I had gotten good at lying to my parents, even though I didn't like it. Throughout college, I had mastered the art of keeping that same boy I met back when I was sixteen a secret. Even at the age of twenty-two, with a degree and a moderately decent job, I didn't feel successful enough to voice that I was in love with a boy who I hoped to marry one day. I felt wrong that I was keeping the biggest secret of my life from my parents. I didn't know if they had changed. I just knew how they originally treated me when I fell in love, and that scared me. Like many South Asians, when you fall in love with a partner, you experience love alone because you are afraid to tell your family. You can't share romantic love with your family; that's not how our culture works. It can be hard and difficult to accept the dishonest child you have become if family means everything to you. That's exactly how I was feeling.

I felt wrong because I felt like being in love was not showing appreciation for everything my parents had done for me. I was at war with my soul, and I didn't know how to process all my feelings. Living back home after college caused me to feel torn. I was trying to figure out my adult identity and assessing if the only relationship I had in my whole life was worth the hassle of expressing myself to my family. I couldn't help how I felt. I really loved him, and I didn't want to keep him a secret anymore. But I couldn't tell them yet. I felt trapped. Feeling trapped created a shadow inside my heart, and the only outlet was my relationship.

I started to examine every aspect of our relationship. I was testing it against my *marriage checklist*. I fought with him tirelessly. I tried to push him away. But everything we talked about only made me love him more. If we were going to get married, we would have an interfaith marriage. We started talking about what that would look like.

Me: *So, if we have kids, what are they going to be? Sikhs? Hindus because you're the boy?*

Boyfriend: *No. We can decide together when we have them. I'm open to whatever you are.*

Me: *Well, I think we should talk about it now because it's a big decision.*

Boyfriend: *Okay. How about we let them choose what they want to practice?*

Me: *But having too many choices can be bad...*

Boyfriend: *Look, if we get married, that doesn't change who we are.*

Me: *If we get married, I think we could practice both of our religions together because, at the end of the day, God is one. Right?*

Boyfriend: *Yeah, I think everyone has the same God. So maybe, they can practice whatever gives them peace. I'm okay with that.*

Me: *So, we're going to let our children pick their religion...how liberal of us.*

Boyfriend: *Who knows what they would like to practice. I don't see why not.*

Me: (smiling) *Okay, I think we can do this.*

Really, though? Could we? Sure, we could get married, but a marriage would be nothing if we couldn't have our families with us to support us in our decision. Our families meant everything to us. Unsure of how to address our love, we kicked the can down the road until we both felt like we were successful enough to present our suitors to our parents.

MENTAL HEALTH IS REAL

EVEN THOUGH I NEVER CROSSED A PHYSICAL BORDER TO immigrate to America, I had mental borders I needed to overcome to really feel seen as an American citizen. I was facing mental battles that I wasn't equipped to handle. Even though I was a "Smart Indian" now, my parents weren't, and I didn't know how to interact with them. When I tried to show them my independence, it was disrespectful. If I tried to correct their thinking or behavior to make them understand how to live a better, more fulfilled life, I was ridiculed. The problem I faced when I moved in with my parents after college had everything to do with upward mobility.

There is a deep feeling of insecurity and guilt you feel when you realize that a few years of college and a degree can give you an instrumentally better life than your parents. This conflict drove me crazy when I saw how our lifestyles were different and how even the way they took care of their lives was different. That difference is a difficulty that cannot be expressed or explained, only deeply experienced with every interaction you have with your parents. Realizing that nothing has changed in their lives, but everything has changed in your life *because* of them is a hard mental health pill to swallow.

People spend their whole lives defining themselves around their problems. While I was soul searching, I realized my problem was that I loved too much. I loved my parents so much that I didn't know how to process and independently be myself. Every thought I had was about them. I associated every happiness I received because of them and not because of my own merit. Every pain I felt was because of them. I had no real sense of identity. Even as an adult, I realized my identity was defined for me. As a woman, I am supposed to care about my family and their honor first. Years of being conditioned to put my family's needs first and mine last was so deeply ingrained in my thoughts that I didn't know how to parse who I was without them. My mental health was so damaged that I couldn't see what my future would look like without my parents.

What deepened my depression was being told that they were my temporary family and that after I got married, my permanent family was going to be my in-laws. They were here to build me up, but they weren't going to be here to ripen the fruits of the tree they had planted. If I told them I disagreed, I was being disrespectful. I told them that just because a daughter gets married, that doesn't mean they lose their right to me. A daughter isn't a temporary guest. She is a permanent resident of the family that she is born to. What I wasn't ready to hear was that I wasn't their investment plan. That there is a reason why Indian parents feel differently about their daughters. It's because it's a fact of life: daughters leave, and sons stay. I wasn't ready to accept that. Being told that I didn't have an obligation to my parents was eradicating the only identity I knew of. I didn't know who or what to be.

The only reality I understood was that I would always be alone. As a daughter, I was alone. I was born alone. I experienced the conditions around my gender alone. I was pushed to outperform my gender to gain affection alone. Even after gaining affection, I didn't know how to accept it. I was reminded of everything I couldn't be and everything my brother was born to be. That hurt. It hurt so much that I spiraled into being a perfectionist. I graduated with my master's before anyone else in my family. I excelled at my job. I did whatever I could to be perfect so that one day, I could finally be heard. I had made it my mission to thrive, not just survive. Not just for myself but also for them.

LOVE MARRIAGE

IT WASN'T UNTIL AFTER I GRADUATED WITH A MASTER'S that I felt successful. I had associated the attribute of obtaining knowledge as being successful, something I learned early on through my father. Having a degree to back my progressive thinking gave me the courage to admit to myself that I was still in love with a boy, and I wanted to call him my husband.

But I didn't have the courage in myself to tell my parents that I was in love. I feared how my accomplishments would be overlooked, and instead, everyone would focus on my emotional side because I was in love. The truth is I never felt like my words alone were enough for me to be taken seriously by my family. My words didn't matter. My thoughts didn't matter. What mattered was what I was able to achieve. I was silenced as soon as I was born, and I grew up accepting that silence as the only reality I had. The only way I could be heard was if I did something that was so monumental that I would be taken seriously. I didn't know my worth. I didn't even know how deeply I was hurting. I had placed my goal so far in the distance that when I finally achieved my self-implicated goal of success, I felt empty. I may have felt different as a person on the *inside*, but on the outside, I was still that voiceless woman who depended on other people to speak for me like armor. I wanted to have a voice, but I was scared. I wanted to scream, but I silenced my own voice. My temporary moment of success was supposed to allow me to finally be me, but I felt powerless.

I created another goal in the future that I wanted to strive toward before I could voice how I truly felt to my parents. *Maybe I can tell my parents after I get into a doctoral program? Maybe they will respect me then because I'll be extremely educated, and there will be no confusion about whether I am stupid in love because I literally can't be stupid. I'll be a doctor in training!* Thinking I had created the perfect plan, I avoided the inevitable ticking bomb that I wanted a love marriage.

What is a love marriage, and why is it called that? In the South Asian diaspora, a love marriage is exactly what it sounds like: a marriage based on love. Your marriage is not arranged, and you do not marry for attributes typically associated with an arranged marriage. In an arranged marriage, you look for traits in a suitor your parents would approve of so you can marry someone exactly like you. Arranged marriages still exist in both America and all South Asian countries. When I was asked throughout school if I was expected to have an arranged marriage, I always said, "No, because my family is American. They aren't just going to pick some random person for me to marry. I get to choose." I was lying, and my reality was entirely that. I was expected to get an arranged marriage or arrange my own marriage by finding someone suitable who would fit the mold of acceptance. I was expected to either find the perfect man who would be accepted by my family or have my parents find that person for me. Being in love with a man who was perfect for *only* me wasn't enough; he needed to be perfect for my Indian family too. The reality in the South Asian diaspora is that we, as individuals, are only as important as our families. There is nothing and no life without family. Everything involves family—providing for your family, continuing your family, being there for your family. If the man I loved couldn't get along with my family, he was no longer an eligible suitor for me. If our families couldn't get along, we wouldn't get married.

For another year, I thought about all the reasons why my family may not accept my love marriage instead of thinking about all the reasons they might. Even though my brother knew about him and had grown to love and respect my boyfriend, he was not my parents; they were different. The truth is my boyfriend had been through every experience with me ever since I was sixteen. He fought for me and loved me when I didn't love myself. He was there for my highest highs (watching me graduate with my college degree alone by sitting away from my family) and my lowest lows (being there for me as I faced every single hardship imaginable). He had been there for everything, but I still couldn't give him the respect and justification he was so desperately seeking: meeting my family so that we could get married.

Part of the reason why I was so uneasy about presenting my boyfriend to my parents was because of the reaction my parents had when they discovered my brother had a girlfriend. It was 2:00 a.m., and I got a phone call from my brother asking me to come pick him up because he had somehow gotten locked out of the parking garage. He instructed me to come alone. I said, "Okay." I tried to sneak out of the house at 2:00 a.m., but I live with my very Indian parents. As I tried leaving, my dad decided that he would go with me because who in their right mind lets their daughter go out alone to the city at 2:00 a.m.? The whole time my dad was asking me questions.

Papa: *Do you know what happened?*

Me: *No.*

Papa: *Was he with a girl?*

Me: *No, with his friends.*

Papa: *Do you know where the garage is?*

Me: *Yes.*

Papa: *Is there anything you know that you aren't telling me?*

Me: *No, Dad.*

As soon as we arrived and my brother got in the car, my brother blurted out.

Papa, mein pyaar ho gaya. (Dad, I'm in love.)

The whole car ride back, I stared at the road as my dad asked my brother a ton of questions. "Who is the girl? How long have you known her? Is she Indian? What kind of Indian is she?" My dad turned to me and asked, "Did you know?" Of course, I said, "No," even though I did. I was never going to snitch out my brother. Our bond was thicker than blood, even if we feuded a million times over.

As soon as we got back home, my dad decided that it was the perfect time to celebrate. He poured himself a shot of Black Label and said, "My son (putar) is in love!" My dad and my brother celebrated that he was in love. Yes, celebrated. Even though I was happy for my brother and that his reaction to being in love was so vastly different from when my parents discovered I was in love at sixteen, that didn't mean it didn't hurt me. It hurt a lot. I became envious. Why was the fact that my brother was in love treated so differently from when my parents discovered that I was in love? Was it because he was older than I had been and had graduated college? Was it because he told them instead of getting caught like I did? Was it because he was a boy, and I was a girl? Why was he being celebrated for breaking the rules and dating a girl, and I was crucified when they found out I dated a boy?

Unable to process my emotions, I grew hatred in my heart for my family. I felt like no matter what I did, I would never be enough. That no matter who I became, I would always be treated differently because I was a girl. I started to be negative, and I started to manifest these negative emotions that I thought my parents were feeling about me into reality. People treat you how you treat them. I started being rude to my parents, yelling after every disagreement, "Is it because I'm a girl?!" I realized I started to find my voice through anger.

A VOICE

I WAS SO ANGRY AT HOW MY FATHER REACTED WHEN HE learned about my brother's relationship that I automatically convinced myself that my suitor would not be accepted by my family. I was constantly fighting my family without even giving them a chance to understand why I was hurting inside. I had accumulated so much hatred in my heart that I didn't even realize that the reason I didn't have my own voice was because I didn't have the courage to speak up. Why didn't I have the courage to speak up even though my family could tell that something was wrong with me? It was because I didn't know how to present my thoughts, feelings, and opinions to my parents without feeling inferior.

And the truth is I really felt inferior. Every time I tried to show them my independence, I was told to comply because that's what women do. Indian women comply with whatever society wants them to become. An outspoken woman is considered rude and someone who doesn't know her place in the South Asian community. I knew deep down in my heart that there was no possible way I could have a calm, collected conversation with my parents about who I wanted to marry without having to compromise every single part of my identity I had worked so hard for. I worked hard to be loved. I worked hard to be noticed so

I could be taken seriously for being more than my gender. But to have to ask for your parents' approval to get married seemed so backwards to me. Why did I even have to do that anyway? Is it because I feel guilty about everything they provided for me? Why couldn't my parents just accept my decision about who I wanted to be with my whole life? I'm an American after all. I don't even need to tell them. I could just elope.

But what I slowly started to realize was that there was no way out. No matter how many times I thought about what would happen if I did tell them, all of these imagined reactions started with one truth: I had to find the courage to tell them, even if I didn't want to. Even though I knew it would take everything in me to have this conversation, I started to realize that the only way out of this was through it. I started talking to my brother and told him how unhappy I was and how I wanted to voice my feelings to our dad. My brother indicated that he could help support me to back up my voice. I agreed because I was scared. My brother and I had a plan; my dad was going to come home, and we both were going to sit down and talk to him about how I was ready to get married.

Days turned into weeks, and then months but my brother and I could never find the right time to talk to our dad together. Growing more impatient each day, I decided, *To hell with the plan.* I decided that nobody knew how to stand up for me the way I needed. Even though my brother wanted to help, I decided to do it alone. I need to believe in myself as much as I wanted my father to believe in my choice. If I got someone else to speak up about the most important decision of my life, how did that make me look? It made me look as if I was weak, and I had something to hide. I had nothing to hide. I had a secure, loving relationship that I felt blessed to have. I was far from being weak. I was only afraid of fear—fear of not being accepted. I was afraid of having to choose between the man I loved and my parents. Yet, the only way forward was to tell my parents; the only way I could get my parents to respect my voice was to speak to up. I had lived a thousand days being silent. Even if I didn't agree with the formal process of asking for permission, I had to meet my dad at his understanding and where he stood in his belief system. I took a deep breath and started walking into the living room where my dad was drinking tea.

Me: *Papa, there's something I need to talk to you about and I need to talk to you about it now.*

He didn't look up at me and continued to sip his tea.

Me: *Papa, it's urgent. Are you free? Can we talk now?*

He looked up. Puzzled but still maintaining his stern demeanor.

Me: *Papa, I found a boy that I want to marry.*

Papa looked away and puts down his tea.

Papa: *Okay, let's talk.*

THE TRUTH

YOU CAN'T TAKE BACK YOUR WORDS ONCE THEY HAVE BEEN said. Once I had spoken the words out loud that I loved a man and I wanted to marry him, the dynamics of my relationship with my parents changed. After I told my dad that he wasn't Sikh or Punjabi, my father needed a moment to grieve the loss of the dreams he had for me. His dream for me was different from mine: he wanted his daughter to marry a man who would be familiar to him. Telling him that I had fallen in love with a Hindu Malayalee South Indian boy brought him to a frightening realization: he had no idea what his daughter was getting herself into, and that scared him.

My mother was upset for a reason that had nothing to do with me: *what would people think about her as a mother?* When a child steps out of the norms in the Indian community, the children's actions are viewed as a real-life example of the mother's parenting skills. She worried about what her family, her community, and even her husband were going to think. The reality of South Asian mothers is harsh. Their whole lives are defined by their children's accomplishments. Their failures are defined by what their children could not do or when they did not fall in line. That experience is magnified for South Asian daughters. They are expected to learn, behave, and marry within the lines of acceptance. When Indian daughters perform out of character or expectations, conflict occurs. That conflict first starts in them (trying to find the appropriate love for themselves) and then in their parents (to accept who their daughter has presented).

After I told my truth to my family, I felt free because there was nothing left to hide. My truth was out in the open, and they had to decide how they wanted to proceed. But all of this involved time, and I was very impatient. I told my parents I wanted to marry a boy who was smart and educated—who came from a good family and treated me like a queen. I expressed that I was happy, and I wanted to share that happiness with my family. But I wasn't embraced with a shot of Black Label like my brother was; I wasn't even hugged. I was told, "We need to think, and you need to give us time to decide." That hurt and made me tunnel down a road of self-doubt.

Giving my parents time to accept my love marriage was the hard part. I didn't care for approval or praise; I just wanted them to accept me for who I was. But I was deeply isolated in my own thoughts about my biggest fear: losing one love (family) for another (my husband). I love my family, but the additional step of approval drove me to the point of insanity. Why did I need approval, but my brother didn't?

To make matters worse, every day, I was growing more and more impatient as I heard nothing but silence from my parents. My mother was easy. She said, "Whatever your father thinks, I'm on board." She indicated that she didn't really have an active voice in this decision and that she supported me always. Unable to come out of her invisibility, my mom let me face my biggest battle alone. My obstacle was my father. He was a strict man, and it was hard to read how he truly felt about anything. Weeks went by, and I still heard nothing from Papa. How could I have a civilized conversation when the only thing that was on my mind was the last thing they wanted to talk about? One day,

I completely broke down. He was trimming the weeds in the backyard, and I asked him.

Me: *So, you're not going to talk to me?*

Papa: *No.*

Me: *Why?*

Papa: *Because you're being rude to the entire family.*

Me: *Why can't we just talk about what I said about getting married? Nobody cared when my brother mentioned something similar.*

Papa: *Stop talking about your brother.*

Me: *It's not fair. It's never been fair. It's because I'm a girl.*

Papa: *Okay, you know everything then. Why are you talking to me?*

Me: *Whatever.*

I ran off. It was literally impossible to talk to my dad and get a straight answer out of him. Unable to handle my grieving heart, I became bitter to the world. To make matters worse, my brother was going to propose to his girlfriend, and the whole family was going to be at the proposal, but I still had no idea how my parents felt about my relationship. To aggravate the situation, my brother was proposing to a woman who was outside of the religion and caste we were. On the day of my brother's proposal, I was filled with mixed emotions. I couldn't help but feel invisible and ignored, even if I was happy for my brother. I couldn't help but feel like my own family had betrayed me.

Feeling defeated, I was going downstairs when Papa called my name as he was shaving with the door open.

Papa: *Sabreet.*

Me. *Yes.*

Papa: *Tell your friend to come to the proposal.*

Me: *What?*

Papa: *Tell your boyfriend to come to the proposal.*

Me: *Um...okay.*

I ran downstairs and immediately texted my boyfriend. "Papa said you can come to the proposal! Can you believe it?!"
My boyfriend responded back, saying, "Are you sure?"
I giggled for the first time in weeks. "Yes, just be there!"

SPEAKING WHAT'S IN OUR HEARTS

HAVING MY BOYFRIEND PRESENT AT MY BROTHER'S PRO-
posal made me feel like maybe my parents were considering
my happiness. He met my parents briefly but stayed to the side
to give my family space. I couldn't help but fall more in love
with him. Here was a man who has been nothing but kind to
my family, and why couldn't they just give him the decency of
a conversation? It was different for me. I had already met his
mother and father, and they were the sweetest people I have ever
met. Even though they were Indian, their ideologies of marriage
were as liberal as mine. Why were my parents taking forever?

A few days after my brother's proposal, I was in my room
trying to ignore the world and find peace in the situation I was
currently in. Someone slid a piece of paper under my door. I
opened the door to see who was there and found no one. I then
bent to the floor to pick up the piece of paper. It was a note from
my dad with an illustration of me. The note said, "You're bad,
but I will talk to him."

I smiled from ear to ear. I ran downstairs to my dad.

Me: *You wrote me a note?*

Papa: *Maybe.*

Me: *So, what should I do?*

Papa: *Tell your friend to come over and have tea with me.*

Me: *Tea?*

Papa: *Yes, tea. I am free tomorrow; he can come.*

I spent all night preparing my boyfriend. I told him to just be himself, and I promised that my dad would love him. The day finally arrived where my suitor came to my house to meet my parents. The twist was that I was not allowed to attend the meeting; Papa wanted to talk with him alone. My whole family was meeting him without me.

Even though I couldn't attend, I felt at ease because I knew my brother would hold down the fort for me. I wasn't supposed to listen to their conversation but sat all the way at the top of the stairs, so they couldn't see me. I heard them talking for what seemed like hours until finally I heard them laughing, and my father told me to come downstairs. I came downstairs, and then Papa asked my boyfriend.

Papa: *So, why do you want to marry Sabi?*

Boyfriend: *Because she's kind, smart, and comes from a good family.*

Papa: *Marriage is forever. If you guys get married, you can't just leave. You stay married forever. We don't believe in divorce. Okay, if I give you my permission, you guys can't just walk away from each other. Marriage is hard, and it takes work each day. You both must promise me you will try your best for each other always.*

Boyfriend: *We will.*

Papa: *Okay, then, you can get married. Now, let's meet your parents.*

Just like that, Papa gave me his approval, but I didn't feel as happy as I thought I would. I was grateful that he approved, but I didn't feel happy.

Feeling confused, I ignored how I felt because I thought I was being a brat. I couldn't shake off my attitude, even though my family approved. I was still short with my family and kept my distance. Pretty soon after my boyfriend met my parents, our parents met, and for the first time in my life, I thought, *Maybe this could work.* I still refused to picture it because I was scared of having the rug stolen from underneath my feet.

My father noticed that I kept my distance and continued to be rude to my family. He called me downstairs to tell me a story.

Me: *Yes, Papa. You called me?*

Papa: *Yeah.*

Me: *What's up?*

Papa: *I just want to talk to you.*

Me: *About?*

Papa: *About your life and why you might feel differently about us.*

Me: *Hmm?*

Papa: *The truth is that daughters and sons are different. They always will be, and you must understand why.*

Me: (annoyed) *Okay.*

Papa: *Daughters are like diamonds. You must take special care of them. Sons are like coal. They aren't as valuable. You're my daughter. I'm not just going to give my diamond to anyone. The reason that Indian families have arranged marriages is to ensure that their daughters will be taken care of and that they are going to be in a good family. In an arranged marriage, someone you trust typically knows that family, and you can trust that they won't hurt you. The problem with arranged marriages is that logic doesn't always work. It doesn't matter if I found you a boy that was Punjabi and of the same caste; that doesn't mean he probably wouldn't hurt you and might not mistreat you. We would have no idea, and you know that our community doesn't believe in divorce. Sabi, the Indian community is really messed up. They actually torture their women and don't care what they have to say. I want to make sure wherever you are going, they respect and care for you like you should be respected and cared for.*

I felt emotional; my eyes teared up.

Papa: *Sabreet, I love you. I didn't know how to love you when you were born. I was upset that you were a daughter. I didn't know how to care for a daughter. I kept thinking about why you weren't a boy for many years. As the years went on, I realized that the biggest blessing I've received is you, just the way you are.*

I was completely crying now.

Papa: *I never want to hurt you. I want to give you your happiness. When I was young, I was in love once too, and I couldn't marry the woman I wanted. My happiness was taken away from me, and the details don't matter now, but I know what unhappiness can feel like. Why would I do that to my own blood? My own soul? Why would I do that to you?*

My nose was running.

Papa: *What I'm trying to say is that I'm upset you didn't come to me sooner. I have been thinking long and hard about trying to find you a perfect husband and I was growing increasingly worried as you aged and matured. There was no way in hell I could find a good husband for my perfect daughter.*

Me: (speechless but trying to respond) *Papa, but how could I come to you? You are strict.*

Papa: *Yeah, I'm strict, but you didn't give me a chance to show you that maybe my thinking has changed too.*

I didn't account for that at all.

Papa: *You want to marry your boyfriend. You know I can't verify what caste he comes from because he's Malayalee. I have no idea if he comes from a good family. I only know what you told me. To protect you from evil, I wanted to be the satellite on earth, looking in every single direction, trying to find you a perfect man. But you found one for yourself. I wish I had been open enough for you to understand that you could have told me.*

Me: *I'm sorry, Papa. I didn't know.*

Papa: *It's ok, beta, just realize that even though it might not seem like it, I'm more open-minded than you think. I love you. I always have. I will always protect you. No matter what.*

He was crying now.

Me: *I love you, Papa.*

Papa: *I love you too.*

When I left that conversation, for the first time in my life, I considered what my father was going through. I had never actually thought about it until that moment. I was so focused and worried about how I was being treated—why my whole life had been different—that I forgot to think about my parents and what their life had been like up to this moment. As an Indian and an American, I had developed two different and distinct identities. What if they were also changing their beliefs because they lived in America? I had never considered that reality because it seemed so far-fetched.

Since so many South Asian parents romanticize the India they left behind, they think back to the India that doesn't exist anymore. When they go back and visit, they know it isn't the same, and they can't help but compare how backwards India is compared to America. Basic human rights don't exist, and sometimes, they feel ashamed to even be considered an Indian. But they aren't comfortable being considered an American either. My parents never voiced those opinions to me. Why would they? There were parts of the American culture they were afraid of. So, they silenced their own growth because they didn't know how it would impact their growing children.

The reason my parents and I butted heads was because we didn't give each other the chance to accept that maybe we were both growing up in different ways in America. And maybe that was okay. To grow, learn from other cultures, and come up with your own belief system is what we were already practicing as a family; we just didn't know how to conceptually talk about it because change is scary. Imagine feeling like you must be this strict parent, even if you don't believe you should be anymore. Imagine feeling scared as a child because you don't know if your true personality can be accepted by your family.

Sometimes, we spend so much time unable to understand our differences within our own family that we don't even give our own blood the chance to be who they want to be. Sure, I wasn't authentically myself to my parents for most of my life. The fear of not being accepted robbed me of years of happiness with my family. It gave my parents years of agony, thinking they were alone in their growing belief system. They were never alone; everything we experienced, we experienced together. Feeling alone made me put up barriers around my relationship with my parents. That barrier was so high that I couldn't climb it to see what was on the other side. When I finally found the courage to climb the barrier to see what was on the other side, I was met with love.

For most of my life, I was on autopilot. I was afraid to speak because I felt voiceless. I believed that reality into existence. You can make anything come to life if you truly believe it. I believed my parents didn't love me because they treated me differently. I believed that I was all alone for most of my life. I believed those things so strongly that I made them into a reality by how I interacted and how I kept those relationships in my life. I was told my gender made my dad upset, so I believed that I could never make him love me. I believed that maybe there really was something wrong with my gender, so I overcompensated and tried to prove everyone wrong. I was living for others, trying to please them and prove them wrong. Every emotion and every decision I made was to prove something to someone. Anyone. I never lived for me. I didn't know how to.

The first person to teach me how to love myself was the man I fell in love with. He encouraged me to find myself. He promised he would always be there, as much as or as little as I needed. He helped me see who I could be if I tried to love myself. I found happiness in being myself around him. But I was afraid to be authentically myself around my family—this new me who actually loved myself. I was conditioned to believe that love wasn't something that is given to you; it is earned or approved. I had to prove myself to be worthy of presenting my love (both the love that I had for myself and the love I felt for this man) to my parents. That assumption hurt me for years. I drove myself to the point of rage, believing I wasn't enough. That they would never love me for me. That the man I wanted to marry would never be accepted. That no matter how hard I tried, my family would regret me.

The truth is what kept me from discovering my own voice was myself. I silenced myself for years because I was afraid of finding the truth. If you don't reach out and talk to the people who are hurting you, they will never know why you are hurting or how they have hurt you. Sometimes, we are so afraid to have a conversation that might end up shaping our whole lives. For me, it was a conversation about love: yearning for unconditional love from my parents, looking for acceptance to show them who I authentically was, and finally presenting to them the man I loved more than anything.

I can't help but wonder...what conversations are you avoiding? That you are afraid to have more than anything? What's always on your mind? Why are you on autopilot? What are you yearning to find? What keeps you up at night? What makes you never be present in your own life? Take a moment and think. What would happen if you had that conversation today? Tomorrow? Where would you be? What would you learn? And what would it ultimately help you realize? People can spend a lifetime agonizing over a moment. Trying to find a simple truth. Why should we spend so much of our lives searching for a truth that's right in front of us? You've already convinced yourself the worst possible scenario of what could happen if you had that life-altering conversation. Why not just take a leap of faith and try today? It may change your life.

AMERICANS, TOGETHER

AFTER MY PARENTS AND MY BOYFRIEND'S PARENTS MET and said they were ready to get us married, I felt awkward. Imagine having lived twenty-six years of your life, knowing that your choice of a life partner must be approved by your family. I spent most of my life fearing and thinking about that approval. I did not know how to process acceptance and genuinely be happy that my parents accepted who I fell in love with. Throughout the course of my life, I had built this fence around my heart, piece by piece. Once I finally had the courage to speak my mind and let my parents inside my fence, I was lost.

I had only practiced multiple scenarios of how to defend my choice. I never once thought about what acceptance would look like because I had no idea what acceptance meant. Having open-minded parents amazed me. Every aspect of wedding planning amazed me because I saw how American my parents were. They started discussing how, after my boyfriend proposed, we could have our Roka ceremony. In typical Punjabi culture, you have a Roka first. A Roka is when all your friends and family come together to bless the couple.

My parents were less concerned about the Roka and more

concerned about the magical American proposal. They had never experienced a proposal before and were super excited to experience it through their children. They knew to keep it a secret from me, but I couldn't help that I was inquisitive. I would overhear my dad talking to his family on the phone, explaining what a proposal was. He indicated that it's when the girl doesn't know, but the guy knows when he is going to propose. Everyone was super concerned—"But what if she says, 'No'?" My dad would further explain that, in an American proposal, the bride and groom have already discussed that they want to be together and have involved their parents, but they wanted to have a private moment where the boy actually asks the girl if she would marry him. Hearing both my mom and dad explain what a proposal was to their respective social circles made me smile. Everyone and everything was coming together; I just had to be present to experience it.

After my extended family learned that I was getting married, the next question was where and how I would get my outfits for both my Sikh and Hindu weddings. Since wedding attire options are limited in America, the obvious answer was to go to India. Getting my wedding outfits from India was a journey but what strikes me the most was how people reacted to me when they found out that I was having an interstate, interfaith marriage.

I remember going to family and friends' homes in India and how awkward it was for them to interact with me. People automatically assumed that I liked South Indian food when I didn't. They would make the biggest effort to either buy Dosa or have someone come into the house and make any South Indian dish, so I could feel at home. Even though I appreciated their gesture, my taste buds hadn't changed because I loved a Malayalee. I still enjoyed Punjabi food. When I went over to people's homes, they gifted me Saris, even though I had never worn one before; as a Punjabi woman, I had grown up wearing a Salwar Kameez.

What I found fascinating about my experience in India was just how afraid people were of change. I went to this one dinner party where a woman sounded concerned after learning about my decision. She had a small young girl, and she reached out to me because she had questions about my love marriage.

Aunt: *So, you're getting married to a Hindu family? Aren't you scared? Isn't it going to be difficult to understand them? They will speak a different language. How will you adjust?*

Me: *Aunt, it's okay—I chose to get married to this man. I love him. I've known him my whole life. He's exactly like me, and we are like a fusion version of Indian Americans.*

Aunt: *What I'm saying is, it will be so difficult for you because they are so different.*

Me: *Not really. We're both Americans.*

Aunt: *The thing is that kind of stuff doesn't happen here. People don't marry outside of their caste, religion, or state. Even if someone wants a love marriage, they know to stay in the lines of acceptance.*

Me: *Auntie, the thing is Indians aren't separated by state, religion, or beliefs there. We are one group because we have every person from every walk of life there. Honestly, I don't even know how I fell in love with an Indian man. In America, falling in love with anyone is possible. That's what makes America... well, America.*

Aunt: *Sounds like something you see in a movie, not something you practice every day. I wish you the best. You seem happy.*

Me: *I am. Thank you.*

For the rest of my time in Punjab, I kept thinking back to the conversation I had with this auntie. Why did she seem so afraid? Why was she so comfortable asking me these questions? Why did she make me feel like I had given myself a death sentence?

On my flight home, I started journaling and thinking about her discomfort, about the questions she asked me. She was clearly looking for answers, and she thought about me because I was putting myself through something that seemed so uncomfortable to her. Why would any logical South Asian woman put herself in such a situation? It was then that I realized that inter-caste, interfaith, interstate Indian marriages aren't prominent in India. To that woman, I was an alien. Nobody like me existed in her immediate vicinity, at least not in Punjab. Even though India is the most culturally diverse place in the world, people resist one another. Each state is its own country with its own belief systems, religions, and cultural customs. No one travels outside of their state unless it is to a modern Indian city for better education or job opportunities. The vast majority of India still stays inside their state borders. Things have been this way forever.

In America, however, it's different: everyone from the different Indian states has the same identity—they are Indian Americans and South Asian Americans together. In America, I intermingled with people from different Indian states all the time. I met them at the grocery store. I saw them at the gurdwara or temple. I became friends with them at school. Everyone who was brown was my family. To imagine that reality didn't exist in India breaks my heart. Imagine how much that country could grow if people looked outside the walls of their own states. It was at this exact moment that I realized my privilege: to be born and raised in a country like America. America helped me see my own people for who they were. Regardless of the color of their skin or what state, religion, or caste they belonged to. It helped me unite a group of people who were unable to see the unity they had in themselves all along.

As wedding planning commenced back home in America, so did my understanding of the community around me. I would overhear my parents explaining my choice of a husband to other South Asian aunties and uncles. They would start by explaining that we live in America, and the beauty of being an American is changing and growing your belief system. Some people understood; some people didn't. Others pretended that they understood, but as soon as they hung up the phone, they would talk about how ridiculous we were. What surprised me the most was the whole process of acceptance. First, I had to present my choice to my parents, and then they had to present my choice to the world. I didn't realize how difficult that would be for them until I saw them do it. Sometimes, my mother would hang up the phone because she didn't care to explain my choices to people anymore. Other times, she seemed defeated. The biggest challenge my father had was his family. Many people on his side of the family did not understand why my father was giving freedom to his daughter. He would explain and argue things to them, but people didn't hold back. They would tell him that he had allowed a darker, intercaste, interfaith marriage, and he should be ashamed of it. What was he bringing into this family, and why? Hearing my dad define my choice to his family and community was admirable and showed me just how much he loved me.

Even though it was hard, I could see how my parents were dealing with and combating the reality that both of their children were having intercaste, interfaith marriages one month apart. Nothing about this new beginning was easy for them or me. Not only did they have to take the time to explain how "progressive" we were, but they also had to worry about funding two Indian weddings, and those are not cheap. Even though it was difficult, it was during this time that we united instead of drifted apart. We had only one thing on our minds: *it's us against the world.*

After the weddings took place, I realized the importance of family. There are customs, rituals, and blessings that come with different relationships. My wedding was a symbol of my freedom—our freedom. We had two wedding ceremonies (Hindu and Sikh) to show that we appreciate everything our parents have done to get us to where we are today. Our families intermingled in the most beautiful way. They embraced different wedding traditions. They smiled when they saw the amount of love our families gave to us. They felt grateful that their children were going to experience a happiness that they never once had for themselves—getting married to their first love.

It's hard being immigrant parents. You watch your children change and grow in so many ways that it inspires you to do better. To be better than who you were yesterday for a better tomorrow. They can't help but think, *Was this the reason we came to America? To experience a sense of joy we didn't even know that we could have?* How would that joy be different if they never left in the first place? Would they even experience joy, or would it be complacency?

South Asian parents that immigrate to America are braver than their kids can ever understand. They took a chance in a new country without really understanding what could even happen. That determination to take a chance influenced every aspect of their lives—how they raised their children, how they grew up in America *with* their children, what values they ended up holding close and dear to their own hearts. Was this being American: to work hard, to find love, to care for your family, and to grow your family by letting a new community member into it? To know what to accept and what to reject? To understand that regardless of our physical differences, all of humanity is just the same on the inside? Was this something America taught them, or was it something that they were teaching America because they believe in giving everyone a chance?

Now, I don't know if America changed my parents or if they changed America. What I can tell you is that I don't know of another country that has this much diversity. Our population has so many different races. America is the only place I know that helps those different races see the similarities within themselves in a way that can't be experienced from their original nationality. America helps people see what's on the inside of every one of us. To be an immigrant is to be an American. It helps you change your thinking, grow your family, raise your children, find happiness, and continue to give back to this country whatever it gave you. For my family, America helped us discover love—the love we have for each other, our community, and our nation. Love has the power to change the reality of every single human being. This country has changed the way my family loves in such a deep way that I can't imagine my life without it. Love saved us. It grows us. It helps us even understand ourselves. America gives us the liberty to love whoever we want. With that liberty comes justice to protect that love, no matter what. After all, anyone who has ever come to America looked for the three uniting things—love, liberty, and the pursuit of happiness.

AUTHOR'S GRATITUDE

THANK YOU FOR READING MY STORY. YOUR TIME AND COM-mitment mean the world to me, and I am grateful to have a reader like you. Thank you. A million times over.

The last page of this book has everything to do with you and nothing to do with me. Writing this book took everything in me. I had to understand where I was hurting, how to heal my pain, and why my truth matters. The truth is it is hard finding your voice. I didn't know I was missing my voice until I realized my whole life revolved around creating the courage to believe in myself—the courage to know that I am enough, that I was born enough, and that I am enough now. I have always been enough; I just didn't know how to see my own value.

Never, ever underestimate your power to be authentically who you were born to be. If you were searching for meaning as you read my story, I encourage you to look within. What are you searching for? Is it causing you pain? Where are you hurting? How long have you been hurting? Are you happy? What is your soul so desperately looking for? I am confident that whatever truth you were looking for in my story is already inside of you. Every nod or moment where you felt like you saw yourself in me, that moment is yours. Look deeply at that moment, and I encourage you to find yourself. Your truth is bigger than mine. *Your voice matters.*

I hope this book gives you the courage to realize that it is okay to speak out about your truth and what it means to have a voice. Women have spent thousands of years being an echo. For as long as human history, women have been afraid to see their own reflections in the mirror, scared to believe in their own power. What if you believed in yourself and your voice as much as you believe in mine? What if your voice is the hero our community so desperately needs tomorrow? Your voice can only come from you if you let it. Maybe I can leave you with the same question I asked myself when I started my journey: *Are you ready to be brave?*

ABOUT THE AUTHOR

SABREET KANG RAJEEV is a first-generation Indian American of Sikh descent. Sabreet is a full-time Social-Science Researcher and holds an MA in Sociology from the University of Maryland, Baltimore County, and a BA in Sociology from the University of Maryland, College Park. She is currently completing her doctorate at the University of Baltimore.

Throughout her life, Sabreet experienced the beauty and struggle of being part of a blue-collar immigrant family, and she is driven to raise awareness and empathy for a minority group of Indian Americans, who do not historically come from educational or economic privilege. *Generation Zero* is her first book.

You can learn about Sabreet by visiting sabreetkangrajeev.com